BELITHA Information LIBRARY

WEATHER
AND
CLIMATE

THEODORE ROWLAND-ENTWISTLE

 **BELITHA PRESS**

First published in Great Britain in 1991 by
Belitha Press Limited
31 Newington Green, London N16 9PU
Copyright © Belitha Press Limited and
Gareth Stevens, Inc. 1991
Illustrations/photographs copyright © in this
format by Belitha Press Limited and Gareth
Stevens, Inc. 1991
ISBN 1 85561 056 6
Reprinted 1991, 1994
Printed in China for Imago

British Library Cataloguing in Publication Data
CIP data for this book is available from the British
Library

Acknowledgements

Photographic credits:

Heather Angel 38 right
Aquila 41 right
British Antarctic Survey 57 right
Biofoto 4
Canadian National 15
John Cleare/Mountain Camera 2 left, 32 left and
    right
Crown copyright 17 top
Department of Electrical Engineering/University of
    Dundee 12
Patrick Eagar 8
ET Archive 37
Sally and Richard Greenhill 5 bottom left
Susan Griggs/Comstock 30, 31
Robert Harding Picture Library 38 left, 41 top, 42
    left, 45, 47 bottom right, 52
Eric and David Hosking 41 bottom left
Huchinson Library 25, 39 left, 51 top, 53
Frank Lane Picture Agency 14/15
G. V. Mackie 17 bottom
Magnum 39 right, 42/43, 51 bottom, 54, 58/59
S & O Mathews 5 top and centre right
NASA 57 left
Oxford Scientific Films 16, 43 right
Panos Pictures 59 right
Photo Library of Australia 36
Science Photo Library 21, 28, 29 right, 33, 34, 35
Charles Tait 47 top
ZEFA 23

Illustrated by: Oxford Illustrators Ltd (Jonathan
    Soffe, Simon Lindo and Ray Webb) and Eugene
    Fleury

Series editor: Neil Champion
Editor: Rachel Cooke
Educational consultant: Dr Alistair Ross
Art director: Frances McKay
Designed by: Groom and Pickerill
Picture research: Ann Usborne
Specialist consultant: Dick File

Contents

Words found in **bold** are explained
in the glossary on pages 60 and 61

1: WEATHER OR CLIMATE?

What's the Difference?

Those Circles

The Equator, the Arctic Circle and the Antarctic Circle are imaginary lines on the map. The Equator joins the points at which days and nights are always of equal length.

The Tropics of Cancer and Capricorn, either side of the Equator, mark the northern-most and southernmost points, respectively, at which the Sun appears directly overhead at the summer solstices.

At the Arctic Circle the Sun does not rise on mid-winter day, and never sets on mid-summer day. The further north you go the more of such sunless and nightless days there are. The Antarctic Circle joins simi-lar points in the south, where the day on which the Sun never sets comes at the same time as it does not rise in the Arctic. ▲

Weather and climate are two ways of looking at changes and variations in temperature, wind, rain and sunshine. The word weather refers to all the day-to-day changes in any particular place. Scientists who study weather are called meteorologists.

The word climate describes the usual weather in that place over a period of years. Scientists who study climate are known as climatologists. They generally regard 30 years as the time needed to work out the climate of a place. But some scientists think 50 or 100 years give a truer picture of climate.

The climate varies from one place to another. We expect long, hot sunny days in summer in the South of France, but in northern England the same summer may be hot or cold, dry or wet. So we say that the South of France and northern England have different climates.

Different Climates

There are even bigger differences if we contrast the climates of the **tropics** (the regions either side of the Equator), and northern Europe or northern North America. The tropics are hot all the year round, with two main seasons, wet and dry. The northern areas have four seasons: spring, summer, autumn and winter.

Changes in Climate

The various climates of the world have changed over the years. Only 20,000 years ago ice covered large areas of Europe, Asia and North America. The ice sheet once reached as far south as the River Thames in England and the Great Lakes of North America.

Climates are still changing now, as you can read in Chapter 5. There are fears that human activity – rather than natural forces – may be causing some of these changes, by burning **fossil fuels** and so pumping huge quantities of **carbon dioxide** into the air.

Politicians and scientists everywhere are now studying the problem to see what we ought to do to halt, or at least limit, these changes. But there are no easy answers as scientists are still uncertain of their causes.

▲ The oak trees in the top picture were photographed at 1.30 p.m. on a grey day in April. The same trees are seen in the lower picture, taken at 8 a.m. the following day: it has snowed in the night – an example of the day-to-day changes in weather conditions.

◀ These two beach scenes were taken at the same time of year but in areas with different climates. The beach on the far left is in Norway, which lies close to the Arctic Circle, while the nearer one is in Sri Lanka, in the tropics.

2: THE WEATHER MACHINE

What Makes the Weather?

► Most of the Earth's water is in the oceans and seas. It moves around the world in what is known as the water cycle. Water from the sea evaporates into the air with the Sun's heat (1) and, as it rises, cools and condenses to form clouds (2). Some of these clouds produce rain (3). If the rain falls on land, eventually the water finds its way back to the sea, for example in rivers (4).

Air pressure

The pressure at any place is the weight of the column of air above that place. The higher above sea-level you are, the less the pressure of the air above you.

When air becomes warm it also becomes less **dense**, and therefore lighter. As a result, changes of air temperature cause changes in pressure and affects the weather. Unfortunately, the atmosphere is so complicated that we can rarely relate changing barometer readings to rising or falling temperatures.

You can think of the weather as being produced by a machine, with the Sun as the fuel driving it and the Earth's **atmosphere** as the machinery.

Just as heat, obtained by burning fuel, drives a car engine or steam turbine, so the Sun heats the Earth's surface and 'drives' its atmosphere. But it does so unevenly.

Because the Earth is shaped like a ball, the heat from the Sun falls most strongly at the Equator, where the heat has least air to travel through and covers the least surface area. Heat falls less strongly at the **poles**, where it is coming at an angle through the air, and therefore through a thicker layer of it, and is spread over a larger area.

Land and Sea

Land heats up more quickly than the sea, and it cools more quickly, too. In the tropics land and sea are always very warm, but in higher **latitudes** (that is, towards the poles) the sea is cooler than the land in summer, but warmer than the land in winter.

This and the more direct heat from the Sun affect the temperature of the air, so there are always areas covered by warm air while others are covered by cold air. When heated air rises, cooler air from elsewhere blows in to take its place. This is the basic cause of the winds.

When the Sun heats the air it also heats the sea, and lifts moisture into the air through **evaporation**. When the moisture-laden air rises high it cools off, and the moisture **condenses**, forming clouds. If the clouds grow cooler, the water in them forms into large drops or **crystals** which fall as rain, snow or hail.

There are definite boundaries between masses of cold air and hot air known as **fronts**. The rising air at these fronts results in clouds and rain. You can read more about them on page 27.

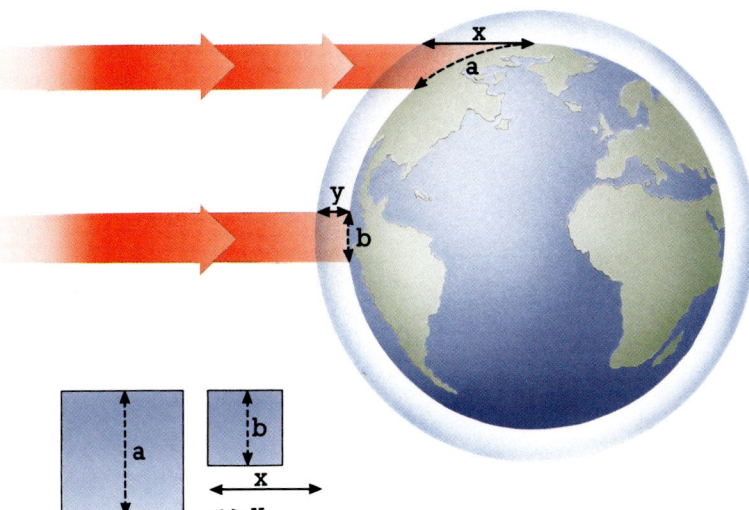

▼ In an aneroid barometer, variations in air pressure cause the disc to expand or contract, so moving the spring and the attached pointer.

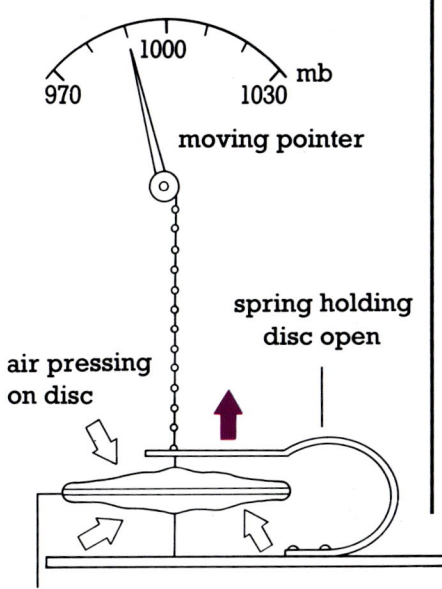

moving pointer

spring holding disc open

air pressing on disc

disc containing partial vacuum

◀ The diagram shows how heat from the Sun falls over a greater area of land at the poles (a) than at the Equator (b). It also has to travel through more air: (x) at the poles and (y) at the Equator.

Clouds

Fog and Mist

Fog forms when water vapour condenses near the ground. It is composed of millions of tiny water droplets much the same as in a cloud. If the droplets form around smoke, chemicals from car exhausts or dirt the result is smog. It often gathers over cities. Fog or smog can make it very difficult to see over more than a short distance.

Mist forms in the same way as fog but is much less dense, so **visibility** is less affected.

▼ During clear, calm nights mist often forms in valleys. It can persist well after sunrise, as in this picture taken in the Vosges, in eastern France.

How They Are Formed

When water is heated it turns into **vapour**, an invisible gas. If you boil a kettle the water is changed into gas rapidly. Water slowly becomes vapour at ordinary temperatures. This is called evaporation. As a result of evaporation, the air often holds a great deal of water vapour.

When heated air rises, it takes water vapour with it. Because the atmosphere is usually cooler the higher you go, the vapour cools, too, and begins to turn back into water – a process called condensation.

The air is full of minute particles of dust and salt, so small that you cannot see them. The water condenses in very tiny drops of liquid or ice crystals around these particles. This is how clouds are formed.

Kinds of Clouds

There are ten different kinds of clouds. They have been given Latin names that describe them. There are three basic types, cirrus, cumulus and stratus.

The word cirrus means a curl of hair, and that is just what cirrus clouds look like – wispy threads in the sky. They float very high, sometimes as much as 10,000 metres above the ground.

◀ Five of the most common types of clouds. From top to bottom, they are the high, streaky cirrus; the patchy grey-white altocumulus; the heavy cumulonimbus (the thunder cloud); the cotton-wool-like cumulus; and the grey, low-lying stratus – shown here hiding the top of the 300-metre tall Eiffel Tower in Paris.

Cumulus means a heap, and cumulus clouds appear as great banks, towering up into the sky. With the Sun behind them they appear dark, but when lit from the front they gleam white. They often form over land on fine days as warm air rises.

Stratus means layer, and stratus clouds form grey layers, usually near the ground.

Two more terms are used to describe clouds: nimbus, which means rain-bearing, and alto which means high. These five terms are combined to name the various kinds of clouds.

The Ten Clouds

Cirrus High, white hair-like clouds.

Cirrocumulus Thin sheets of cloud forming ripples or very small patches.

Cirrostratus Almost transparent, whitish cloud, often causing haloes around the Sun or the Moon.

Altocumulus Grey-white cloud in sheets or patches, often in small rounded masses.

Altostratus Grey, streaky cloud, often thin in places, which may cover the sky completely.

Nimbostratus Thick cloud, often dark, blotting out the Sun and generally producing rain or snow.

Stratocumulus Rolling masses of grey or whitish cloud with dark patches.

Stratus Generally grey, low-lying, uniform cloud, often producing drizzle; hides hilltops and even the tops of skyscrapers.

Cumulus Detached heaps of cloud, rising into domes; sometimes looks like lumps of cotton wool.

Cumulonimbus Heavy, towering cloud, with a mushroom top and a dark base; the thundercloud.

▼ A rainbow forms when the Sun shines on raindrops in the sky. Each raindrop acts as a tiny prism, breaking the sunlight into the colours of the spectrum – violet, indigo, blue, green, yellow, orange and red.

Rain, Hail and Snow

Size Facts

Raindrops vary in size. The biggest are those that fall in a summer thunderstorm. They may be as much as 8 mm across. The smallest drops are those found in drizzle, which are 0.5 mm or less across.

The biggest snowflakes are up to 50 mm across. Those are the very wet ones which fall when the temperature is rising. Hailstones mostly vary between 6 and 12 mm, but some are more than 50 mm across. The heaviest hailstones reported fell in Ohio, USA in 1981. They weighed up to 13.6 kg.

Meteorologists use the term **precipitation** to describe all the forms in which water falls to the ground from clouds. They have made a list, used internationally, of eleven different kinds of precipitation. But for most people there are just three: rain, hail or snow.

They all start in much the same way, by the tiny cloud droplets or ice particles joining together. It can take one million droplets to form one raindrop. Some cloud particles are water, some are crystals of ice – depending on the temperature at which they form.

How They Fall

As the droplets grow bigger they become heavy enough to fall to the ground. Ice particles may melt and fall as rain if the air is warm enough, but if the air is cold they probably fall as snow or hail. Snow is much more common in cold winter weather. Hailstones, because they are heavy and fall rapidly, can reach the ground still frozen in spring or summer.

Rainfall is measured in millimetres with an instrument called a rain gauge. The heaviest rainfall is in the tropics. The great heat of the Sun there draws large amounts of water up to form clouds. Rainfall in the tropics often averages over 2,500 mm a year. In the **temperate** lands of the north rainfall is much lower.

There are huge differences in the amount of rain even in a small **land mass** like Britain. In the south-east the rain may be less than 500 mm a year, while high mountains in the west can have ten times as much.

▲ Snowflakes form many different patterns, but they always have six-sided symmetry.

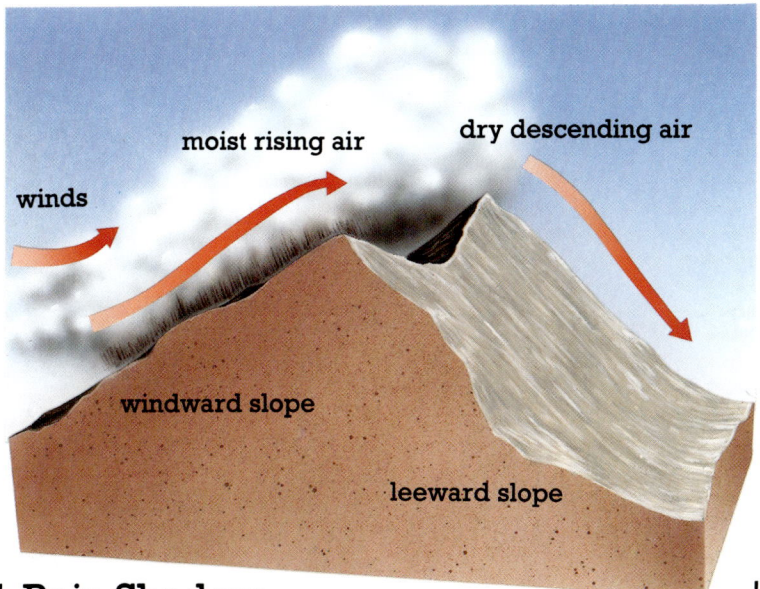

Rain Shadow

The west of Britain is wetter because most of the rain-bearing winds come from the Atlantic, and shed their rain on the western slopes of the **Pennines** and Welsh and Scottish mountains. The eastern side is in what is called a rain shadow.

A similar rain shadow is cast in the opposite direction by the Great Dividing Range of Australia, leaving much of the interior of that country a desert.

Dew and Frost

At night, when the Sun is no longer warming the ground, plants and other objects on the ground may become so cold that water vapour in the air condenses on them. If the vapour condenses as water, we get dew. If it condenses as ice, we have frost.

You can often see frost on the grass or on windows early in the morning. This is because they became cold during the night. Any vapour that touches these very cold surfaces turns to ice.

◄ When moist air is forced to rise to cross mountains, it forms deep clouds and rain falls on the mountains' windward side. The air that descends is less moist and the leeward side of the mountains is warmer and drier – it is said to be in a rain shadow.

Did You Know?

Rain sometimes falls from a cloudless sky. The reason for this is that the cloud has dispersed before the rain from it reaches the ground.

Wind, Highs and Lows

▶ This picture taken from the US weather satellite NOAA-9 shows two depressions (lows) over western Europe – they are the swirls of cloud over the North Sea and Sweden. The cloud spirals are caused by the way the winds blow around a low. These winds would be very strong and the weather bad close to the low.

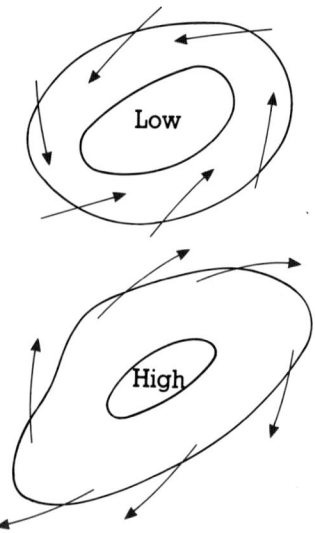

▲ The diagram shows how, in the northern hemisphere, winds spiral anticlockwise around an area of low pressure and slightly inwards. Around a high, they spiral clockwise and slightly outwards.

The variations in air pressure described on pages 6-7 are the key to understanding the world's weather. When warm air rises the air pressure at ground level is lower. Wind blows inwards towards centres of low pressure. But, because the Earth is spinning round on its **axis** from west to east, the wind is diverted. In the northern **hemisphere** the winds blow off course to the right, and in the southern hemisphere they curve to the left.

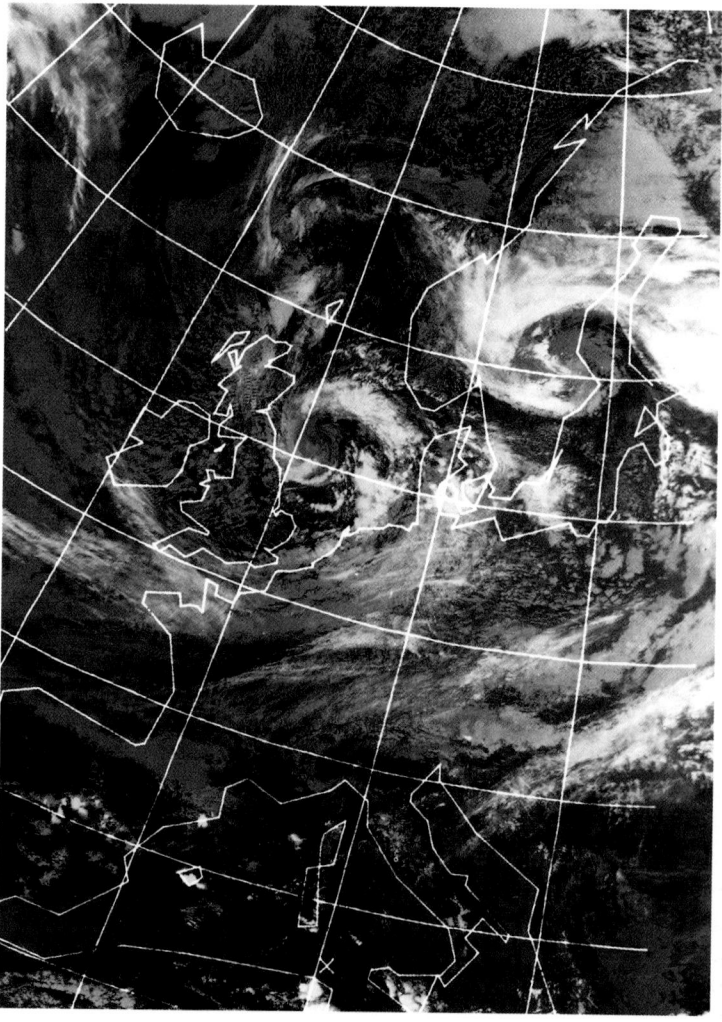

In the northern hemisphere, the wind blows round a centre of low pressure in an anticlockwise direction. From a centre of high pressure, the winds blow slightly outwards and around in a clockwise direction. These directions are reversed in the southern hemisphere.

Fine Weather or Clouds

Centres of low pressure are called **cyclones** or **depressions**, or just **lows**. Centres of high pressure are called **anticyclones**, or **highs**. Lows are nearly always accompanied by heavy clouds and strong winds, while highs have only a little cloud and light winds. So in a high you can expect fine weather. In a low the weather may be dull, wet, and even stormy.

Veering and Backing

The wind does not blow evenly. Friction with the Earth's surface makes the wind gusty. Gusts are very local, and places as close as 100 metres apart may have very different winds at the same time.

When the wind is gusty it generally changes direction. It can either veer – that is, change its direction clockwise – or back – that is, change its direction anticlockwise.

On land in the northern hemisphere, winds tend to increase and veer during the day, and decrease and back during the night. They change less over the open sea. In the southern hemisphere these changes of wind direction act in the opposite sense.

▼ By day the heat of the Sun warms the air over land causing it to rise and allowing cooler air to blow on shore. High up there is a weak flow of warm air in the opposite direction (dashed line). At night the land becomes colder than the sea and wind blows from the land to the sea.

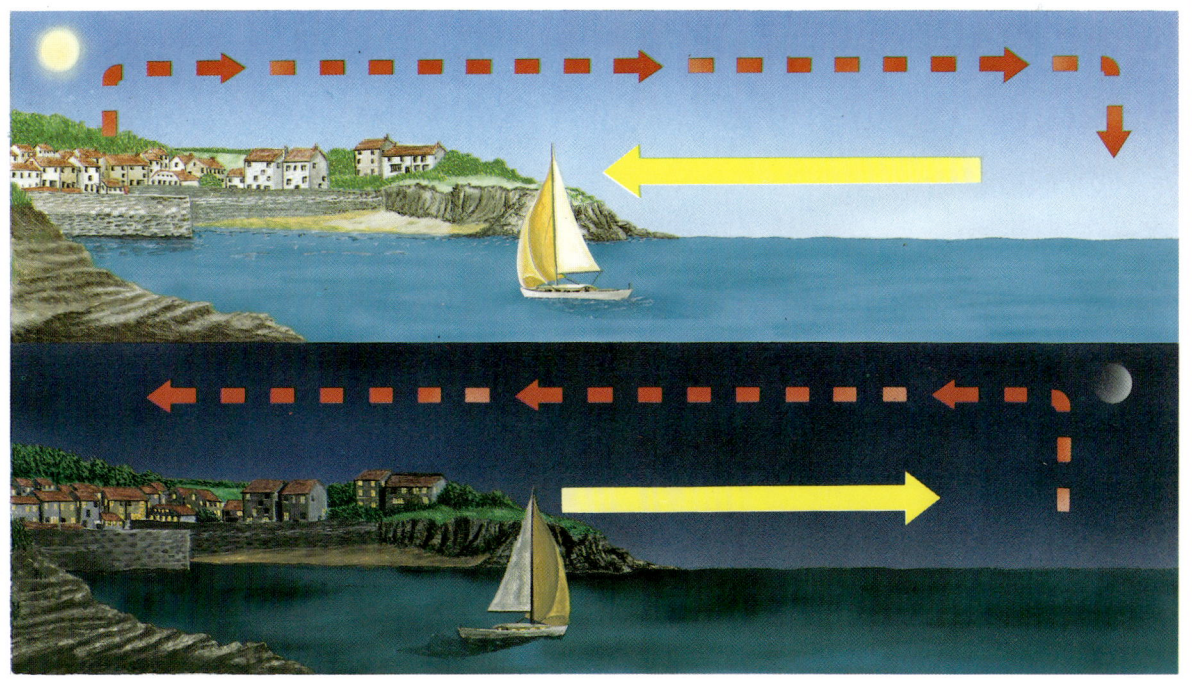

Storms

▶ A tornado causes terrible damage, and can pick up and carry large objects for a long way.

▼ Diagram of a tropical storm – in reality about 500 km across. Rising air in the cloud (1) draws in a rush of air lower down (2) while the 'eye' (3) remains calm. Winds spiral out at high levels (4).

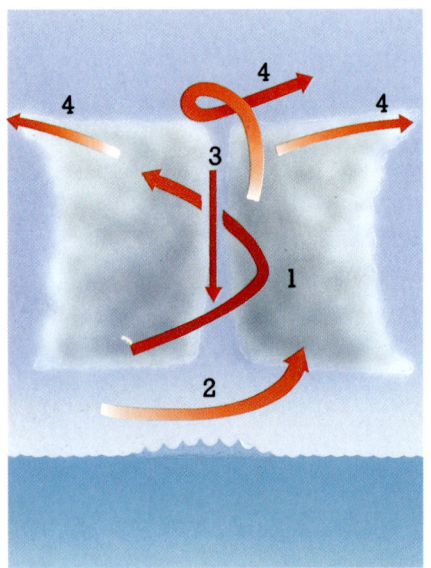

Did You Know?

The worst tropical storm ever to be recorded hit Bangladesh on 12-13 October, 1970. It killed about a million people. The worst tornado to hit the United States killed 689 people in Missouri, Illinois and Indiana on 18 March, 1925.

The strongest winds occur as a depression develops. Air is sucked into the low at or near ground level, whirled round and upwards, and hurled out of the depression high above the ground. The deeper the depression, the more violent the winds become, and a storm blows up. The word storm implies a severe gale but can also be used to describe a thunderstorm.

Tropical storms

The most violent weather is met in tropical storms. They develop over the sea, but may drift over land. They are most common in three regions of the world.

In the Caribbean Sea and the southern part of the North Atlantic Ocean, they are called **hurricanes**. In the Indian Ocean area, they are known as cyclones (Australians call them willy-willies). In the North Pacific Ocean, the Japanese name them typhoons.

A tropical storm may be hundreds of kilometres across. At the edge of the storm the

▼ Lightning hits the CN Tower in Toronto, Canada.

winds are probably around 32 km per hour. As you get nearer the centre of the storm the winds become more and more violent, and may exceed 200 km per hour. Right in the centre there is a complete calm, the 'eye' of the storm.

A Trail of Destruction

Over land tropical storms do tremendous damage, destroying trees and crops and wrecking buildings. On coasts they whip up huge waves which smash on shore, where they cause flooding and kill many people.

More violent winds are met in tornadoes, but they are much smaller, only 350 metres wide on average. A **tornado** is a funnel of wind whirling around at about 300 km per hour. It usually has a dark thundercloud overhead.

As the whirling funnel rushes along, it sucks up everything in its path, even buildings, like a giant vacuum cleaner. A tornado can do even more damage along its track than a hurricane. Many tornadoes occur over the United States which suffers about 830 a year.

3: WEATHER FORECASTING

Reporting on the Weather

In order to forecast what the weather is going to be like, a meteorologist has to know what it's doing now, and where it's doing it. To find this out a series of observations has to be collected from a wide area. They must all be made, as nearly as possible, at the same time.

The further ahead the forecast, the bigger the area from which observations must be collected. For example, a forecast for any part of the world for three or four hours ahead needs information on the state of the weather up to 500 km around.

If the forecast is for three or four days ahead, observations for the whole of the hemisphere are needed.

▶ An American ground hog, or woodchuck. Its shadow is said to be a clue to when winter will end.

16

Taking a Global View

Weather systems are moving about all over the globe, affecting each other. If a northern meteorologist is trying to forecast the weather more than five days ahead, information from the southern hemisphere is needed. Beyond ten days it is almost impossible to forecast: too many unforeseen changes can take place.

What has to be observed? The forecaster needs information on the wind, temperature, air pressure, **humidity**, clouds, precipitation and visibility. The observations are easy to make, and anyone can set up and operate a simple weather station.

The reports come from a variety of sources. Human observers provide the main facts, and they are backed up by reports from automatic weather stations, ships at sea, airliners in flight, automatic **weather buoys**, **radar** stations, equipment carried aloft by balloons, and photographs taken by satellites.

▲ The picture shows various thermometers inside a box called a Stevenson screen, part of a simple weather station. This stands 1.2 metres above the ground and provides shade and good ventilation for measuring temperature.

▼ A weather ship monitors changes of temperature, wind, humidity and air pressure. This is the appropriately-named *Cumulus*.

Radar, Balloons and Satellites

Radar scanners are constantly sweeping the skies to pick up information about clouds and rain. They can detect the difference between heavy and light rain.

Weather balloons filled with **hydrogen** or **helium** carry instruments called sondes. They sample conditions high above the ground and give a three dimensional picture of the weather. The balloons radio information back to the ground. Their position is tracked by radar. When a balloon reaches a height of roughly 30 km it bursts because the pressure outside is less than that inside the balloon, and the sonde parachutes back to the ground.

Space Watch

The first weather satellite, the United States' Tiros I, was launched on 1 April, 1960. Since then a network of satellites has been built up to keep a continuous watch from space on how the Earth's weather is behaving.

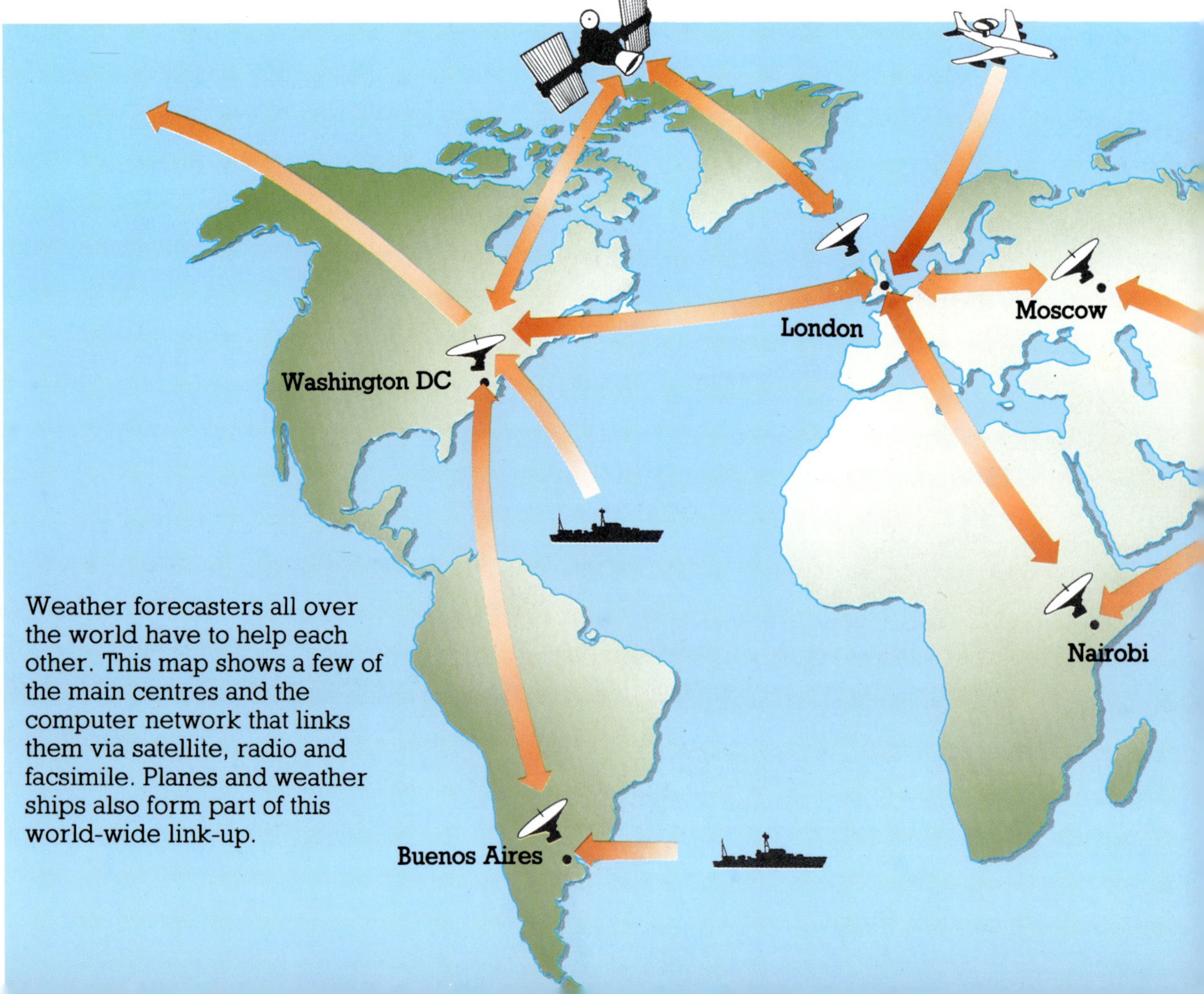

Weather forecasters all over the world have to help each other. This map shows a few of the main centres and the computer network that links them via satellite, radio and facsimile. Planes and weather ships also form part of this world-wide link-up.

Moscow

London

Washington DC

Nairobi

Buenos Aires

Some satellites go around the Earth taking pictures all the time; others may take a picture every 30 minutes. A satellite beams pictures to a command station on the ground, where the outlines of coasts are added by computer. You can see them as white dotted lines in television statellite pictures.

The command station beams the amended picture back to the satellite, which relays it to receiving stations all over the area it covers.

Keeping in Touch

In this way a weather satellite acts as a communications link as well, but ordinary **communications satellites** are needed to send pictures and **data** from faraway stations.

Weather information is no use unless it can be gathered quickly. Local information is needed in about half an hour, and even material from the other side of the world must arrive within three to six hours to be helpful.

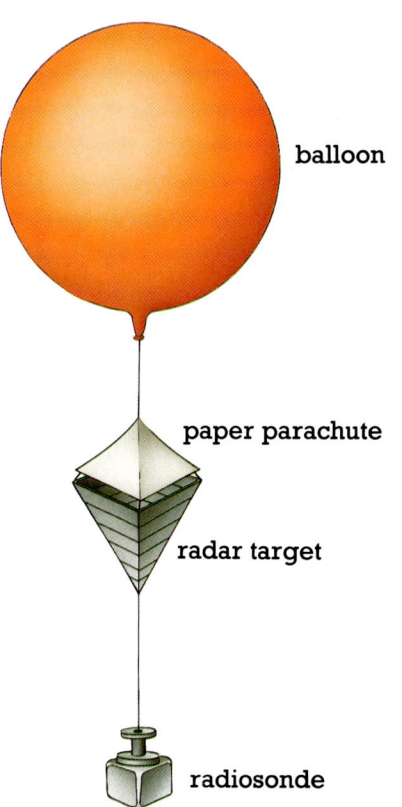

balloon

paper parachute

radar target

radiosonde

▲ A weather balloon carries a sonde, an instrument that monitors weather conditions high above the ground and radios the information back to Earth. Its radar target enables it to be tracked from the ground. When the balloon finally bursts, the paper parachute allows the equipment to float down gently. If the sonde is recovered it can be used again.

Tokyo

Delhi

Melbourne

Computer Link-Up

The quickest way of communication is by **computer networks**, which can send and receive huge amounts of information quickly.

All the world's major meteorological centres are linked by computer hook-ups.

Putting It All Together

▶ This flow chart shows how all the information about the weather is gathered together to bring you the daily forecast.

▼ Points of equal pressure are plotted on a map and then linked by lines called isobars.

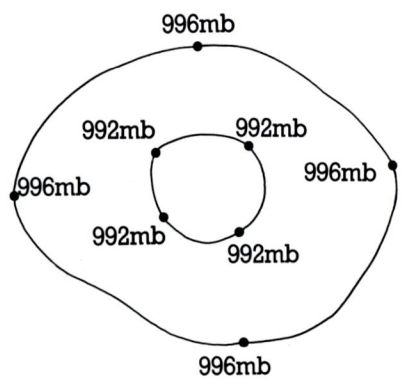

Human beings can work out a reasonable forecast over a limited area for up to 18 hours ahead. But for larger areas and for longer periods the task is so complicated that computers must do a lot of the work.

Very powerful computers are needed. For example, the British Meteorological Office uses one that can perform over one billion calculations a second.

Mathematical Calculations

The keys to most forecasts are highs and lows. The way in which they move indicates changes of wind direction, which in turn may produce changes of temperature. The computer works all this out and prints out a chart, with the probable pressure patterns marked on it. The chart is marked with an international code so that other countries can use it, too.

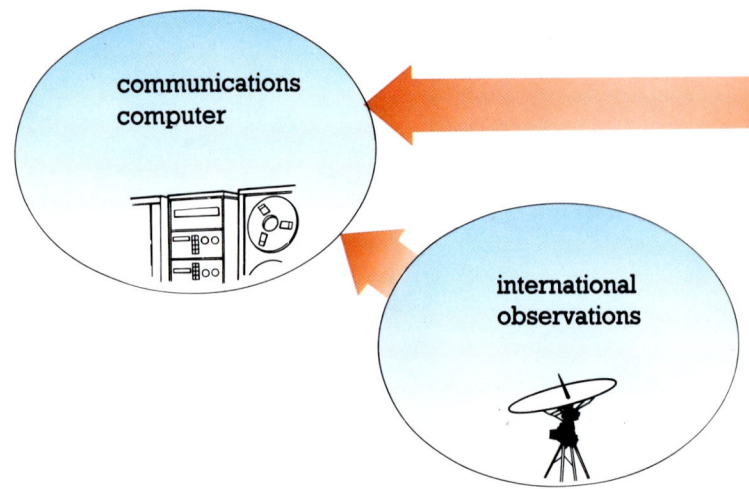

Pressure Points

Next those swirling lines are added to the map. These are **isobars**, from the Greek word *isos*, meaning equal. Isobars link points where the pressure, expressed in bars, is equal. They're similar to the **contour lines** on a geographical map, which link points of equal height.

Having studied the chart, and compared it with a series of satellite pictures showing the recent movement of clouds, the forecaster has to decide what is likely to happen.

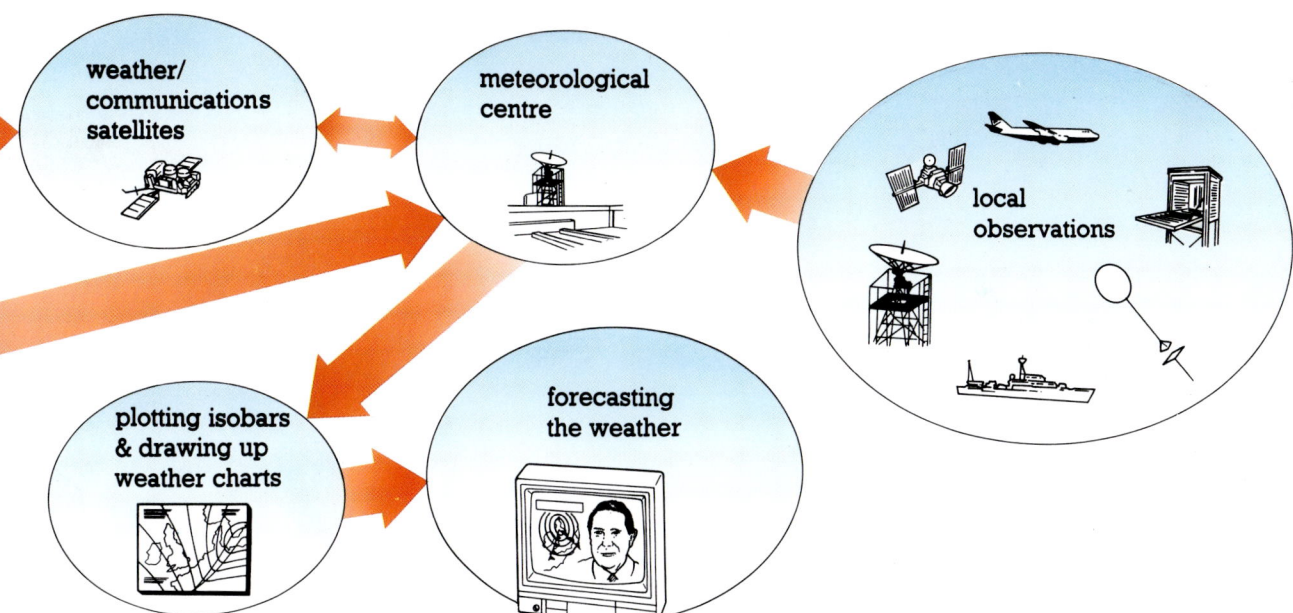

weather/
communications
satellites

meteorological
centre

local
observations

plotting isobars
& drawing up
weather charts

forecasting
the weather

It's not easy: the weather seems to change course as unpredictably as a group of children running around a school playground! In fact forecasts are right a great deal of the time. When they seem to be wrong it's often a matter of timing: it's hard to predict the speed at which a weather system is moving so rain doesn't arrive when it is expected but turns up hours earlier or later.

▲ Top; a weather forecaster at work, surrounded by banks of computers and VDUs (visual display units), which show all the information that is coming in from around the world.

Reading a Weather Chart

▶ This chart shows a typical weather pattern from north-western Europe, with isobars and observations plotted, which the key helps us interpret. In the west, there are clouds, rain and showers, along with high winds around the area of low pressure and its associated **fronts** (see page 26). But in the east, high pressure leads to clear skies – apart from where light winds enable mist to form. Wind speeds are measured in knots, which are nautical miles per hour.

At first sight a weather chart may look complicated, but the signs and symbols on it are really very precise. Even the charts that meteorologists use themselves, which contain much more detail than the charts you see in newspapers or on television, can be read quite easily with practice.

The first things to look for are highs and lows. Even if they are not labelled, you can pick them out by seeing how close the isobars are. If they are close together you are probably looking at a low, where pressure changes rapidly. You can expect high winds and rain with a low.

Highs have widely spaced isobars, and generally indicate clear weather. In winter they may indicate frost or fog.

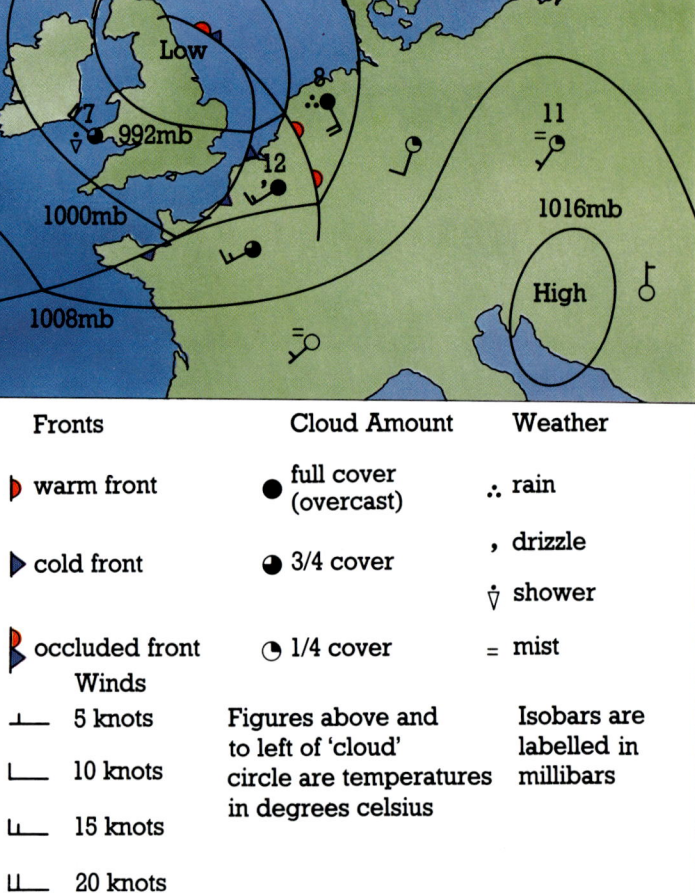

Fronts	Cloud Amount	Weather
▶ warm front	● full cover (overcast)	∴ rain
▶ cold front	◗ 3/4 cover	, drizzle
▶ occluded front	◔ 1/4 cover	▽̇ shower
Winds		= mist
└─ 5 knots	Figures above and to left of 'cloud' circle are temperatures in degrees celsius	Isobars are labelled in millibars
└─ 10 knots		
└� 15 knots		
└L 20 knots		

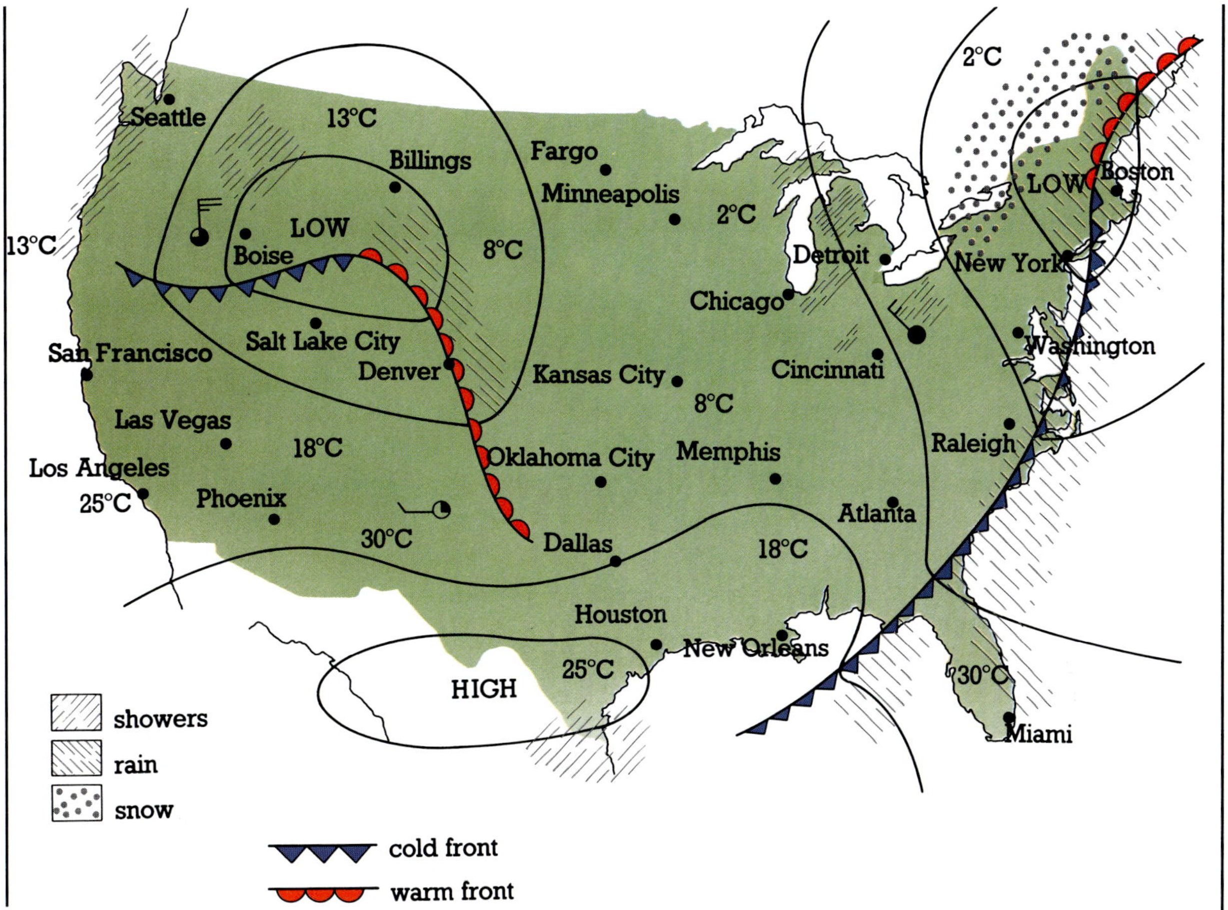

Seattle
13°C
Billings
Fargo
Minneapolis
2°C
13°C
LOW
Boise
8°C
Detroit
New York
San Francisco
Salt Lake City
Denver
Kansas City
Chicago
Cincinnati
8°C
Las Vegas
18°C
Oklahoma City
Memphis
Raleigh
Los Angeles
25°C
Phoenix
30°C
Dallas
18°C
Atlanta
Houston
New Orleans
HIGH
25°C
30°C
Miami
2°C
LOW
Boston
Washington

showers
rain
snow

▼▼▼▼ cold front
●●●● warm front

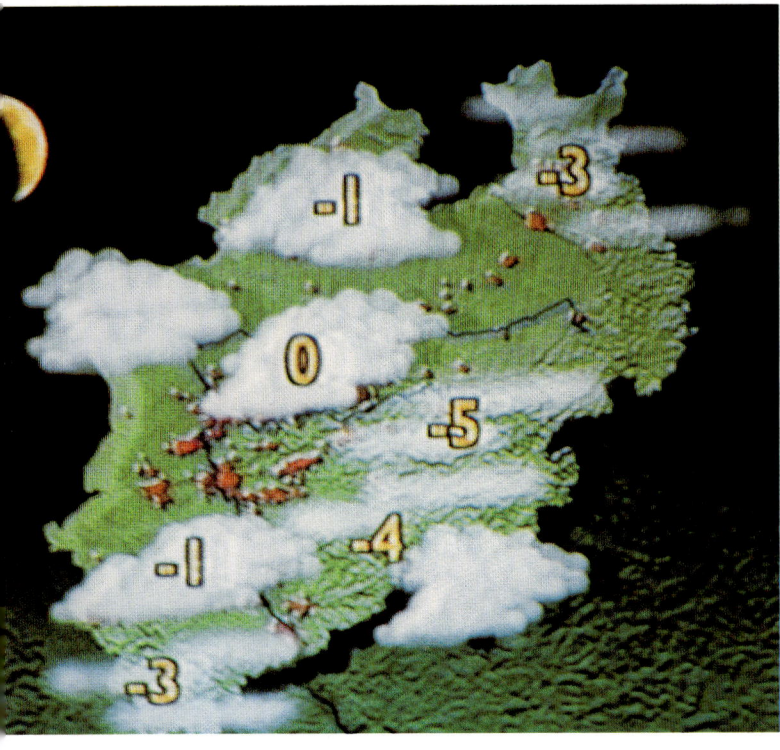

▲ A weather chart for a day in April in the United States, showing some very mixed weather over a wide area. The east coast has rain associated with a cold front. There is snow in the north-east associated with low pressure and a warm front, and temperatures are not far above freezing. Over the south-west is an area of high pressure, with temperatures as high as 30°C – very warm indeed. Moving north-west, the weather becomes cooler, with rain along the warm front and showers further north. High winds, caused by low pressure, are indicated by the plotted observation west of Boise.

◄ TV weather maps, like this one for a region in Germany, are even simpler and a forecaster explains them.

4: | CLIMATE

The World's Climates

The Climates

Icecap Always below freezing; sometimes snows.

Polar Cold, with a short chilly summer; little precipitation.

Subarctic Long cold winters and short cool summers; light to moderate precipitation.

Steppe Great changes from hot to cold except near coasts; little precipitation.

Highlands Always cooler than surrounding climate zones.

Continental moist Cold winters, warm or cool summers; moderate precipitation.

Oceanic moist Cool winters, warm summers; moderate precipitation.

Desert Great changes from hot by day to cold at night; little precipitation.

Subtropical dry summer Mild, wet winters and hot dry summers.

Subtropical moist Cool winters, warm to hot summers; moderate precipitation.

Tropical wet and dry Hot, with a dry season and a very wet one.

Tropical wet Hot and wet all the year.

Many of the important differences in the world are due to varying climates. They affect the kinds of plants and animals that flourish. They also help shape the landscape.

Climate affects people. It influences the way they live, dress and work. It even changes their bodies, because over thousands of years people have altered **genetically** to suit the part of the world they live in.

Many climatologists agree on twelve basic different climates. Present-day scientific

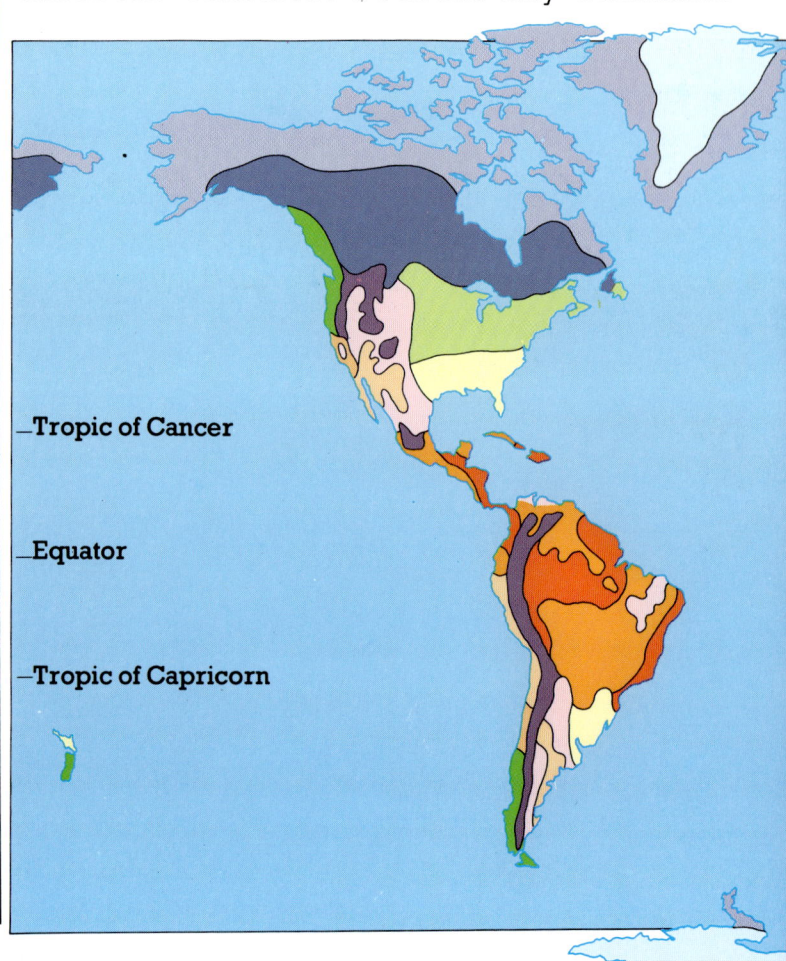

—Tropic of Cancer

—Equator

—Tropic of Capricorn

methods, using **statistics** and information from satellites, have produced other ways of classifying climates, but the twelve are a useful working list for everyday use. You will find them in the panel on the opposite page.

Climates range from cold and dry at the polar **ice caps**, through hot and dry in the deserts to hot and wet near the Equator. Within each climate area there are many variations. For example the British Isles are in the oceanic moist zone, but the Highlands of Scotland have much more rain than south-east England, and tend to be colder.

Kenya lies in the tropics with the Equator running through its centre. As you might expect, the coastal region around Mombasa is hot and humid, but the highlands around Nairobi are a good 9°C cooler, while the highest mountain in the country, Mount Kenya, has glaciers on its upper slopes.

▲ Mount Kenya lies almost on the Equator, but it is always capped with snow and has glaciers on its slopes. With the warm grasslands below it, we see how there can be variations within one climate area.

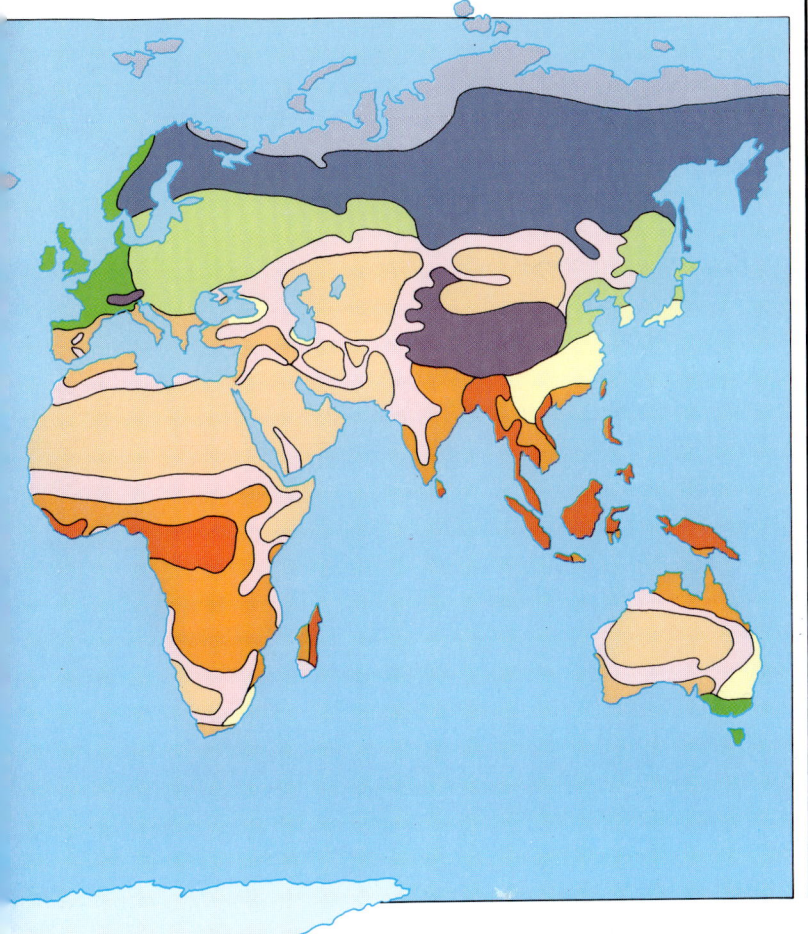

Protective Skin Colour

People who live in places with hot climates, such as Africa, the Pacific Islands and the Mediterranean area, tend to have dark skin. They have developed genetically so their skin contains extra melanin, a dark **pigment** which helps to protect them from the harmful ultraviolet rays of the Sun.

◄ This map shows the world's climatic regions. There is a key to it far left. Although the equatorial region receives most heat from the Sun, you will see that the main areas of desert lie well to the north and south of the Equator. The climate of western Europe, oceanic moist, is matched only in a few other areas of the world.

Sea and Land

The sea covers nearly three-quarters of the Earth's surface. It stays at a more steady temperature than the land and has a marked effect on climate. Coastal areas have less variation in temperature than inland ones. This influence is made stronger by ocean currents.

Most surface currents are caused partly by the rotation of the Earth, and partly by the wind, which drives the surface water along. Some are produced by the effect of **tides**.

Currents flow deep in the ocean as well as on the surface. These flow from the cold polar regions towards the warmer Equator.

The Gulf Stream

Ocean currents affect the weather and climate of coastal regions. The Gulf Stream is a well-known warm current which takes some of its water from the Gulf of Mexico. It eventually becomes the North Atlantic Drift Current which crosses the North Atlantic Ocean to warm the shores of the British Isles, Norway and Iceland.

▼ The map shows the world's principal warm and cold sea currents. Their basic cause is the movement of cold water from the poles towards the Equator at depth, and the movement of warm water near the surface, away from the equatorial region.

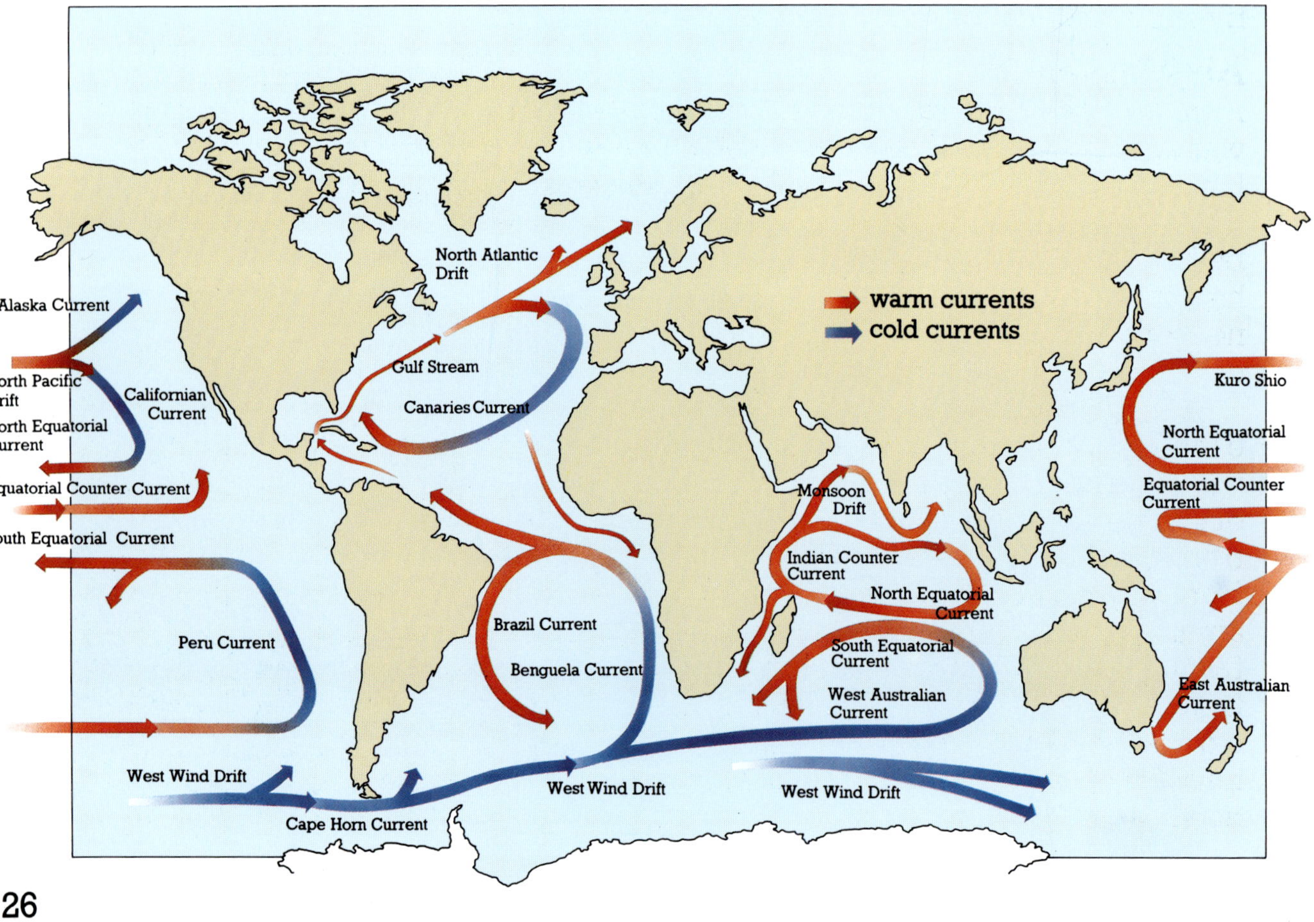

➡ warm currents
➡ cold currents

Alaska Current

North Pacific Drift

Californian Current

North Equatorial Current

Equatorial Counter Current

South Equatorial Current

Peru Current

West Wind Drift

Cape Horn Current

North Atlantic Drift

Gulf Stream

Canaries Current

Brazil Current

Benguela Current

West Wind Drift

Monsoon Drift

Indian Counter Current

North Equatorial Current

South Equatorial Current

West Australian Current

West Wind Drift

Kuro Shio

North Equatorial Current

Equatorial Counter Current

East Australian Current

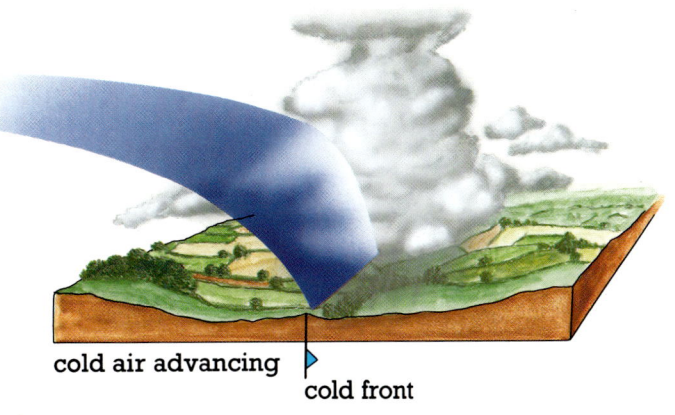

cold air advancing

cold front

Which Direction?

If people talk about the direction in which an ocean current flows, they always refer to the direction *toward* which the current flows. Thus a southerly current flows from north to south and a northerly current from south to north. But see the box about the winds on page 29.

warm air advancing

warm front

warm air

cold air

cooler air

occluded front

The greatest land masses – Europe-Asia and North America – heat up well in summer and become very cold in winter. For this reason, vast areas of Siberia and Canada are covered by snow and ice for many months of the year.

Air Masses

A southerly wind in Europe will usually be warm as it carries air from across the Sahara. Large volumes of air, known as **air masses**, move around the world in this way. They can be hot or cold according to where they are, or have recently been. An air mass that has been near the Equator is warm, while one that comes from the poles is cold.

The boundary between two air masses is called a **frontal zone**. Some frontal zones are very marked, while at others the temperature of one air mass shades into the other. Where a frontal zone reaches the ground we have a front. Fronts are always on the move. If warm air is pushing out cold air we have a warm front. If it is the other way round we have a cold front. And if the warm air is pushed above the cold air, so that the cold front lies between two masses of cold air, the front is said to be **occluded**.

▲ The diagram shows the weather patterns associated with cold, warm and occluded fronts, and the symbols used to represent them on a weather chart. A cold front brings clouds and rain but once it has passed through the rain usually stops. As a warm front advances, the clouds get lower and rain or snow may fall. An occluded front is more complicated – it may bring rain but the weather pattern is harder to predict.

El Niño

El Niño is an unusually warm current which affects the Pacific every two to seven years around Christmas – El Niño refers to 'The Christ Child'. It blocks the flow of rising, plankton-rich water from the Antarctic, in which fish thrive, up the west coast of South America. Fishermen cannot make their usual catches.

The World's Winds

▶ The world's major wind zones. The horse latitudes and the doldrums are regions of calms, where there is usually little or no wind, though there may be sudden storms.

▲ An anemometer on the top of a tower at Jodrell Bank Observatory in northern England. The radio telescope in the background is one of the largest in the world.

Although there are many local winds, which may blow for a day or two at a time, there are certain major wind zones in the world. They are known as **prevailing winds**.

For just over a thousand kilometres either side of the Equator, where the temperature is generally highest, there are no prevailing winds. This region is known as the doldrums, a name which seems to come, appropriately, from 'dull'.

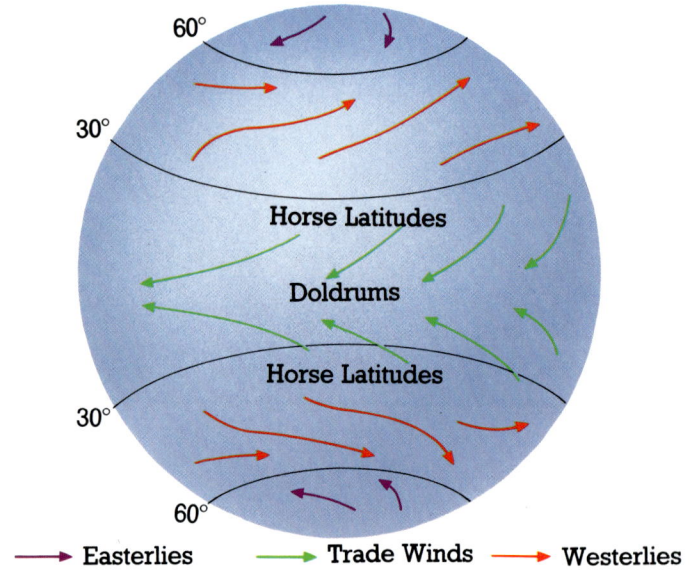

→ Easterlies   → Trade Winds   → Westerlies

The Trade Winds

Either side of the doldrums are the two regions of trade winds. They blow towards the Equator, and slightly from the east because of the rotation of the Earth. Their name comes from the days of trading ships sailing around the world, which relied on them for power.

At a distance 30° latitude either side of Equator is another belt of calms. They are known as the horse latitudes, possibly because on long voyages in sailing ships any horses on board were likely to die of thirst when a becalmed ship's water supplies ran low.

North and south of the horse latitudes are the prevailing westerlies, the winds which in the northern hemisphere bring western Europe weather from across the Atlantic Ocean. They usually blow slightly away from the Equator,

◀ Strong prevailing winds can leave trees permanently bent, like these examples, where the wind generally blows from the right of the picture.

but are very variable from day to day. Finally, around the poles are the prevailing easterlies, which blow slightly outwards from the poles.

Measuring the Wind

Wind speeds are measured by various instruments. The most common is the anemometer. This instrument has three, four or six cups on spokes, which whirl round and round. The wind speed is calculated from the speed at which the cups revolve.

▲ Clouds in a jet stream over Egypt and the Red Sea photographed from the US spacecraft *Gemini 12*.

The Beaufort Scale

Wind speed is indicated by a series of numbers from 0 to 12 (17 in the United States). It is called the Beaufort Wind Scale after its English inventor, Rear-Admiral Sir Francis Beaufort.

No.	Name	Speed km/h	Effects
0	Calm	Under 1	Smoke goes straight up
1	Light air	1-5	Smoke shows wind direction
2	Light breeze	6-11	Wind felt on face
3	Gentle breeze	12-19	Leaves move, flags fly out
4	Moderate breeze	20-28	Dust and small branches move
5	Fresh breeze	29-38	Flags flap, small trees sway
6	Strong breeze	39-49	Large branches sway
7	Moderate gale	50-61	Whole trees sway
8	Fresh gale	62-74	Walking into the wind is difficult
9	Strong gale	75-88	Chimney pots and tiles blow off
10	Whole gale	89-102	Worse damage, trees fall
11	Storm	103-117	Very heavy damage
12-17	Hurricane	over 117	Buildings wrecked

Jet Streams

Jet streams are currents of air high above the ground – usually at between 9,000 and 15,000 metres. They travel at speeds up to 400 km per hour. If an aircraft flies near or in them its speed is affected.

There are five main jet streams. One just north of the Equator travels, in summer only, from east to west. The other four jets flow from west to east, two in each hemisphere.

Strong jet streams occur near fronts and depressions. When high, fast-moving cloud can be seen, changeable weather is often on its way.

Why Do the Seasons Occur?

▼ ► The changing seasons have a dramatic effect on plant life in temperate regions. In these two pictures from New England the fresh green colours of the trees in early summer change to the rich reds and golds of fall (autumn), just before the leaves drop off for the winter.

To understand the seasons, you have to know something about how the Earth moves. It goes round the Sun, like a ball being whirled round and round your head on the end of a string. It takes a year to complete the journey.

At the same time, the Earth is spinning round once a day on its own axis, like a bicycle wheel on its axle. But the Earth's spin is not parallel to the line it takes round the Sun. It is tilted at about $23\frac{1}{2}°$.

As you read on pages 6-7, the Sun heats the Earth more strongly at the Equator than at the poles. You can see on the diagram how different parts of the Earth receive more sunlight at certain times of the year than at others.

Summer and Winter

When the North Pole is tilted towards the Sun, the northern hemisphere has summer, and the southern hemisphere has winter. When the South Pole is tilted towards the Sun, the southern hemisphere enjoys summer and it is winter in the northern hemisphere.

The tropics, the region between the Tropic of Cancer and the Tropic of Capricorn, have very much the same amount of sunlight all the year round. They do not have summer and winter. Instead they have a wet season and a dry season.

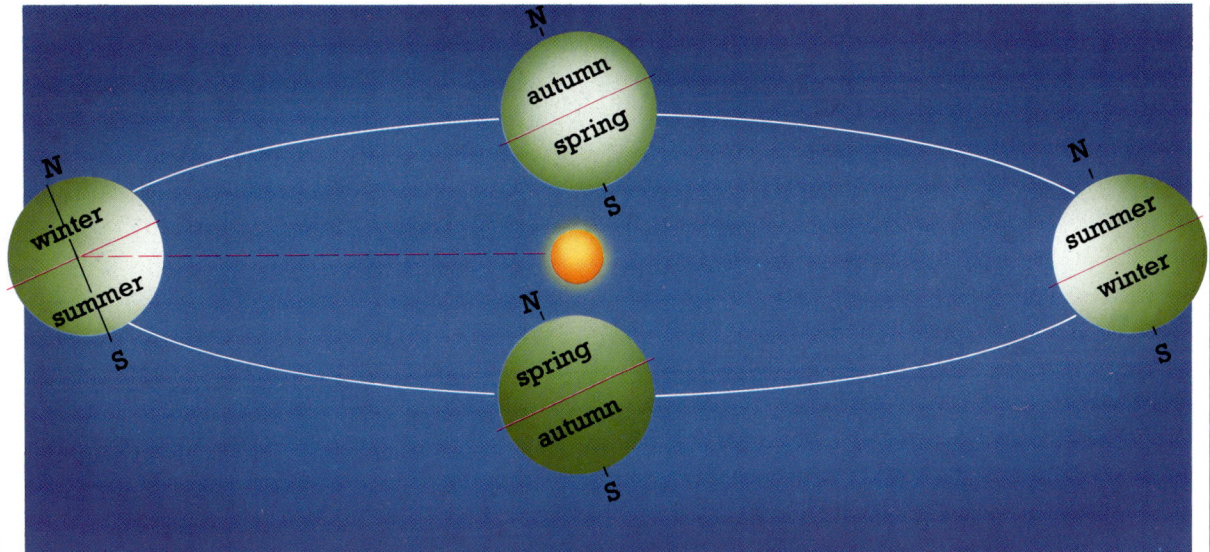

If you look at a map you will see that most of the world's land lies in the northern hemisphere. Because of land's rapid gain and loss of heat, the northern half of the world has more extremes of temperature and more varied weather than the southern half.

Day and Night
The rotation of the Earth causes day and night. At the Equator, day and night are almost equal. Further north and south, days are much shorter in winter and longer in summer because of the Earth's tilt. Longer nights help to make the weather colder.

▲ Places on the Earth receive differing amounts of sunlight during the year because the Earth's axis (line of rotation) is tilted at an angle to its path around the Sun. This produces the seasons. When it is summer in the northern hemisphere it is winter in the southern hemisphere, and vice versa. There are more hours of daylight in summer than there are in winter.

What Makes a Climate?

▼ North and south facing slopes have different climates, as shown by these two views, taken on the same day in late summer, of the *Brèche de Roland*, a pass in the Pyrenees. Left, the slope on the northern, French side is still covered in snow, despite the time of year. Right, on the southern, Spanish side there is not a hint of snow.

There are many reasons why climates vary from place to place. Like the weather, climates are the result of the Earth's surface being heated by the Sun, and cooling down at night. The movement of the world's ocean currents also affects climate.

A tiny amount of heat comes from inside the Earth, but hardly enough to influence climate. However, the Earth gives off heat that it gains from the Sun. The gains and losses vary from place to place. The resulting effect – that is, the overall loss or gain of heat – is called the **radiation balance**.

Gains and Losses of Heat

The first thing that influences these gains and losses is the latitude of a place – where it is north or south of the Equator. As you saw on pages 6-7, the surface of the Earth receives most sunlight near the Equator, and the amount gradually gets less towards the poles.

The atmosphere acts as a buffer both for incoming and outgoing heat. Locally, cloud cover makes a big difference, and so does the

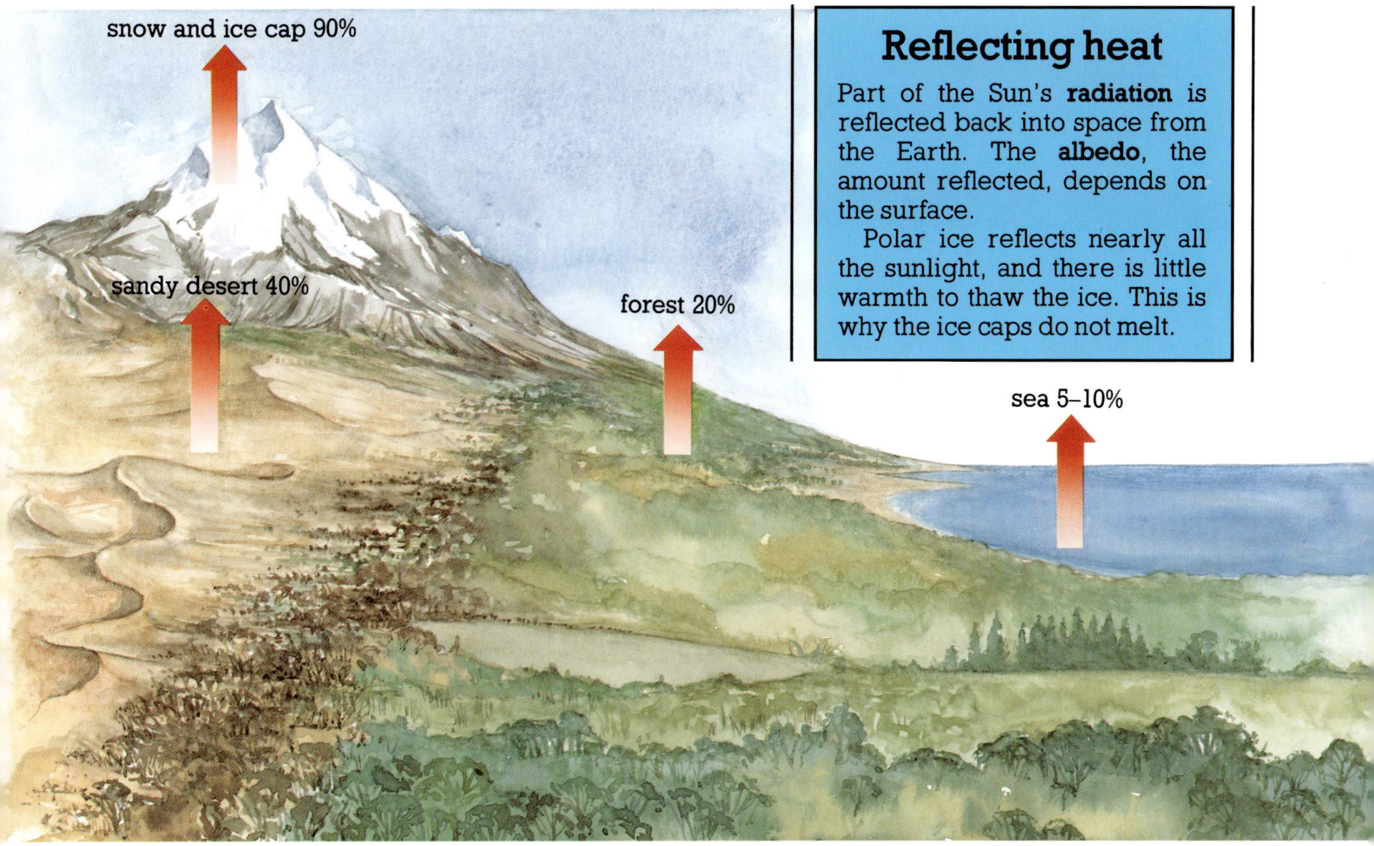
snow and ice cap 90%
sandy desert 40%
forest 20%
sea 5–10%

Reflecting heat

Part of the Sun's **radiation** is reflected back into space from the Earth. The **albedo**, the amount reflected, depends on the surface.

Polar ice reflects nearly all the sunlight, and there is little warmth to thaw the ice. This is why the ice caps do not melt.

amount of soot and other pollutants in the air. The Sun never shines so brightly through an industrial haze as it does where the air is clear.

The sea is the great storehouse of water. It is also a reservoir of stored heat, which is why coastal areas tend to have more moderate climates than places in the middle of continents.

The wind is funnelled by mountains and valleys, and even by buildings. The direction in which the wind blows and where it is coming from affect the temperature and rainfall.

North and South Facing Slopes

A lot depends on which way the land slopes. Ground facing south in the northern hemisphere, and north in the southern hemisphere, receives more sunlight than the opposite slopes. The extra warmth and light means that plant life has a greater chance of flourishing on these slopes. Many farmers use this knowledge when planting their crops.

▲ This shows the percentage of the Sun's light and heat that is reflected by different surfaces.

▼ An experimental solar power station in Sicily. The Sun's heat is so intense it can be used to generate electricity.

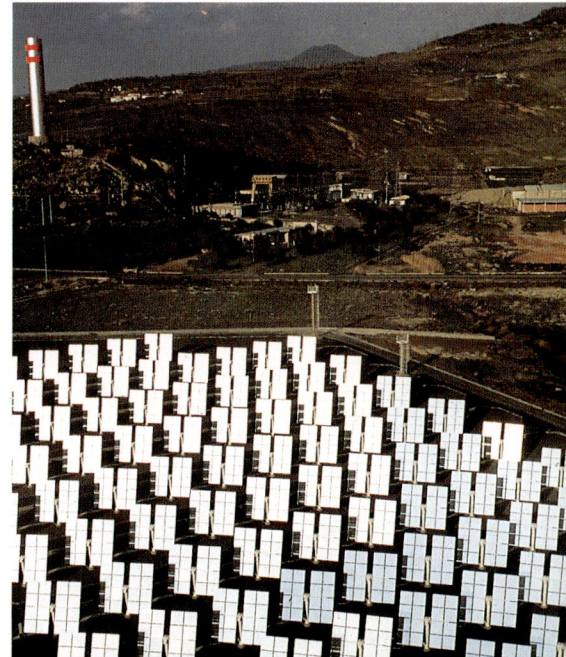

The Unquiet Sun

▼ This exaggerated diagram shows the Earth's elliptical orbit and its nearest and furthest distances from the Sun.

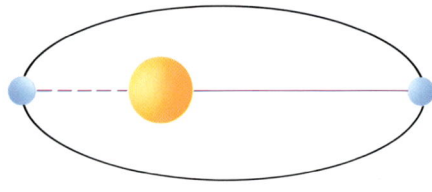

--- distance at perihelion
— distance at aphelion

▶ This picture gives an idea of the constantly changing surface of the Sun. It shows a solar prominence, a loop of gas which may reach 32,000 km above the Sun's surface. This one erupted for over two hours and was photographed in December 1973 from the US space station *Skylab*. The gas was glowing at a temperature of 20,000°C, with some strands reaching about 70,000°C – water boils at a mere 100°C.

The Sun is not a steady source of heat, like an electric fire. For one thing, the Earth's position in relation to the Sun is always changing.

The Earth's **orbit** around the Sun is not a circle, but an **ellipse**, in effect a squashed circle. The Sun is not at the centre of the ellipse, but slightly nearer one end of it.

When the Earth is nearest the Sun it is said to be at perihelion (from Greek words meaning 'near the Sun'). When it is furthest away it is at aphelion ('from the Sun'). The difference between perihelion and aphelion is more than 4,000,000 km. The Earth's tilt in relation to its path round the Sun varies over many thousands of years, changing the climate.

Sunspot Activity

The Sun pumps out a continuous stream of electrically-charged particles, which is called the **solar wind**. The force of the solar wind varies, like that of a hosepipe when the water is being turned up and down.

The solar wind reaches its peaks during **sunspot** activity, and especially when a **solar flare** occurs towards the end of a spell of sunspot activity.

Sunspot peaks occur about every 11 years, and reach their biggest peaks about every 22 years. These periods vary at times and may be as close as nine years or as far apart as 14.

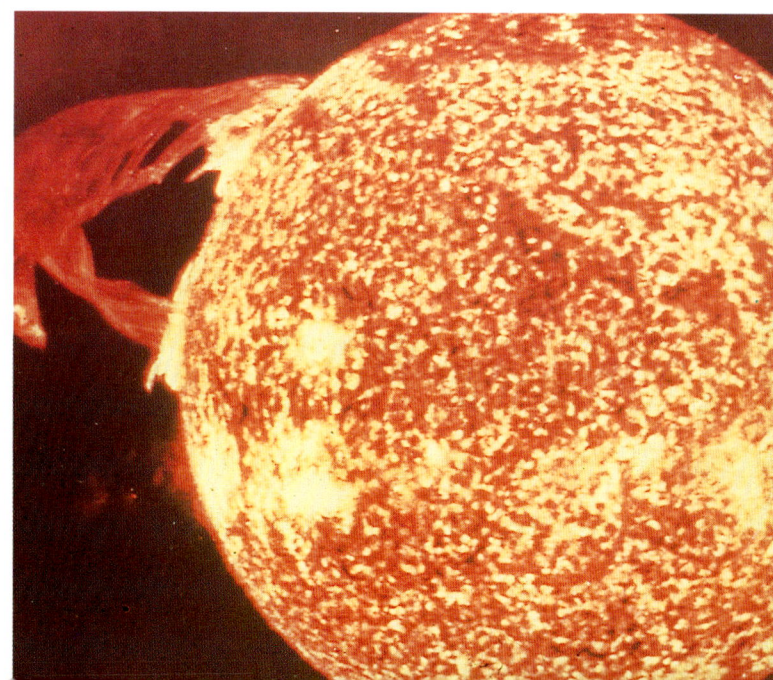

◄ The aurora borealis, or Northern Lights, photographed over spruce trees near Fairbanks, Alaska. These strange lights are caused when electrically charged sub-atomic particles (that is, particles smaller than an atom) from the Sun act on atoms and molecules in the Earth's upper atmosphere. They occur between 100 km and 1,000 km above the ground. These auroras are concentrated over the North and South Poles by the Earth's magnetic field.

Sunspot Facts

Sunspots are dark patches which appear from time to time on the Sun's surface. The Sun is a huge ball of burning gases, a vast nuclear furnace. It has a **magnetic field**, like a gigantic bar magnet, and sunspots are the result of changes in the magnetic field.

When sunspot activity is greatest we see auroras, the flickering lights in the sky in the far north – called the aurora borealis or Northern Lights – and the far south – the aurora australis. Sunspots also lead to radio and TV interference and upset magnetic compasses.

Warning: Never look at the Sun without special apparatus; you could be blinded. Smoked glass is not enough to save your eyes.

Why There Is Less Rain

Statistics suggest that there is reduced rainfall just after periods of great sunspot activity. There are some indications that sunspot 'super peaks' occur about every 90 and 200 years, producing changes in climate.

Tides on Earth are caused by the pull of the Moon, and extra high tides are the result of the combined pull of the Moon and the Sun. In turn, the planets cause tides in the gases which make up the Sun. So since what happens on the Sun affects our climate, climatologists need to study events in space to find out what is happening, or likely to happen, on Earth.

Volcanoes and Meteorites

▼ Scientists believe that this huge crater at Gosse's Bluff, in Australia, was made by a comet which collided with the Earth millions of years ago.

▶ When a volcano erupts it sends a stream of red-hot lava pouring down its sides. Lava is the erupted form of magma, the molten rock that exists many kilometres down inside the Earth. A volcano also hurls forth a cloud of ash, gas, steam, dust and lumps of rock.

When dirty factory chimneys and car exhausts pump fumes and soot into the air they produce a haze. The same thing happens on a gigantic scale when a volcano erupts.

Mount St Helens in the United States blew up in 1980 and hurled about 2 km³ of dust into the air. Volcanic dust is very fine indeed. You could line up about 20,000 dust particles side by side along 1 cm space of your ruler. Imagine how many particles there are in 2 km³.

The Mount St Helens eruption was by no means the largest known. Cosigüina in Nicaragua in 1835 produced about 20 km³ of dust. Volcanoes put forth huge quantities of the gases **sulphur dioxide** and carbon dioxide.

Scientists think that the combined effects of volcanic eruptions over the years have a cooling effect on climate, at least temporarily.

Missiles from Space

Very large **meteorites** from outer space can produce even bigger dust storms. A number of prehistoric meteorite **craters** have been identified, such as the Barringer Crater in northern Arizona, which is 1,265 metres in diameter. That is small compared with the 442-km wide depression identified in the 1950s on the shore of Hudson Bay, Canada.

The Hudson Bay crater may have been produced by a collision with an **asteroid**, one of the host of tiny planets which orbit the Sun midway between Mars and Jupiter.

A collision of that size could put up a cloud of debris which would blot out sunlight for several years, killing plants and animals. Such a collision may have been the cause of the extinction of the dinosaurs.

Near Misses

There have been at least two near misses with asteroids in recent years: Hermes, which is 1.6 km across, missed Earth by only 800,000 km in 1937 – about twice the distance from the Earth to the Moon – which is very close in the vastness of space, and in 1989 another asteroid came within 1,600,000 km.

◀ One of the many dramatic sunsets painted by Joseph Turner, who lived from 1775 to 1851. This one was probably painted at Rouen, France.

Those Turner Sunsets

The dust veil from a large eruption may persist for years, producing spectacular sunsets. It is thought that the dramatic sunsets painted by the 19th century British artist Joseph Turner were caused by volcanic dust, possibly from Cosigüina.

Climate and Plants

▲ Tundra and alpine vegetation near a lake in Alaska.

▲ Coniferous forest, found mostly in cooler lands.

▼ Equatorial and tropical rain forest, found in hot lands.

coniferous forest

Mediterranean scrub

temperate broadleaved forest

equatorial and tropical rain forest

grassland

semi-desert

desert

tundra and alpine

ice desert

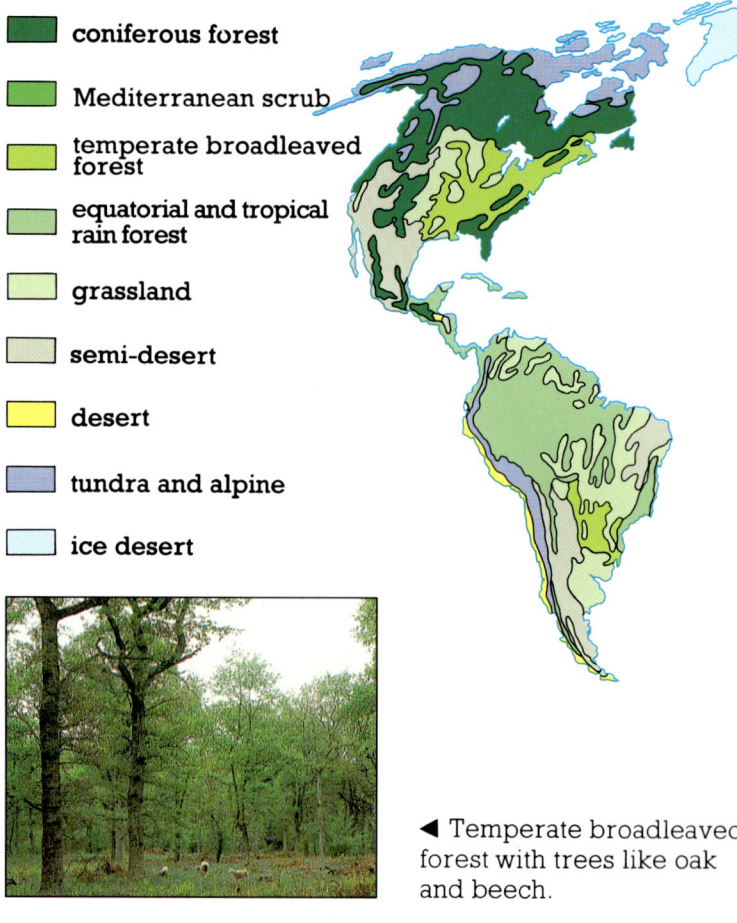

◄ Temperate broadleaved forest with trees like oak and beech.

Climate determines what plants can flourish in an area, and therefore what animals can live there. For example, in the tundra of the far north summers are short and winters are long, with snow covering the marshy land. No trees grow in the tundra, which lies north of the **tree line** – roughly the line of the Arctic Circle.

The only plants that can survive in the tundra are small low growing species. Mosses and **lichens** flourish, and other plants have a very short flowering season. Migrating animals move to the tundra in summer to graze.

The Frozen South

Antarctica, the frozen southern continent, lies almost completely inside the Antarctic Circle. Mosses, lichens and just three kinds of flowering plants grow in a few places near the coast. About 50 species of extremely tiny insects, spiders and other creatures survive there.

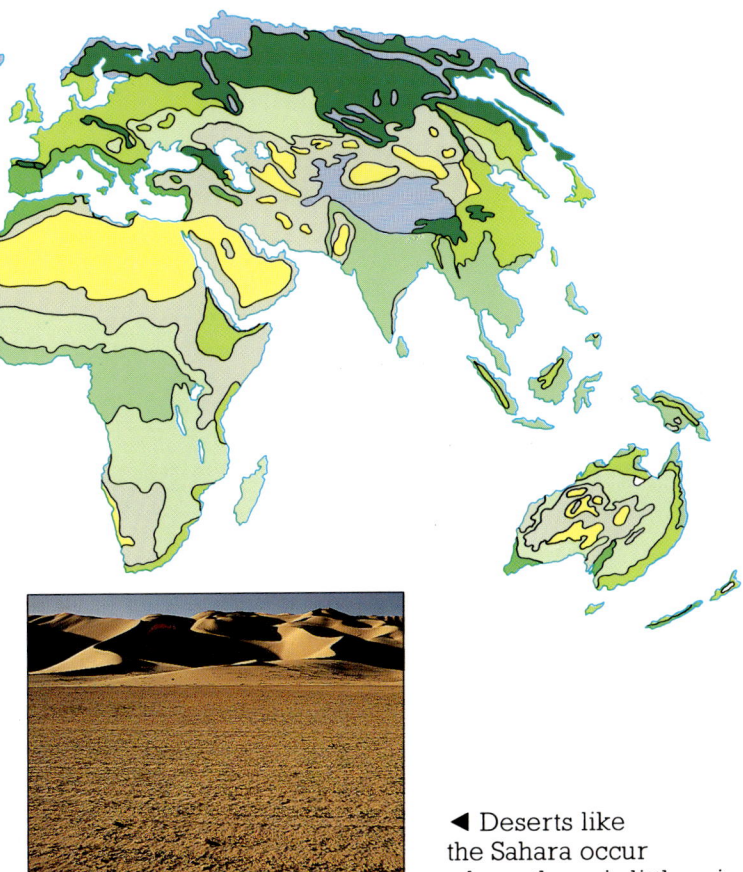

▲ Ice desert in Greenland, where little or nothing grows.

▲ Grassland flourishes where few trees can grow.

◄ Deserts like the Sahara occur where there is little rain.

In the temperate regions of the world, between the Arctic and Antarctic circles and the tropics, there are forests of broad-leaved trees in the warmer areas. There are also wide grassy prairies.

In the tropics, where the climate is warm and wet, forest trees grow to great heights. This region has the largest number of different plants and animals in the world.

The Higher, the Colder

Altitude can have the same effect as moving to the north or south, because the higher you go, the colder it becomes. The high **Himalayas** are snow-covered all the year round, even though they lie at the same latitude as North Africa and Florida, and enjoy the same amount of daylight.

A mountain also has a tree line. Its height above sea level depends on the climate in which the mountain is found.

▲ Semi-deserts have a few hardy plants such as giant cacti.

▲ Mediterranean scrub, also called maquis.

Climate and Animals

▼ Many animals make their homes in burrows under the ground. Some do so to hide from predators and, in cooler climates, for warmth. But others, such as this North African jerboa, or desert rat, live underground by day to protect themselves from the burning rays of the Sun. They come out to hunt in the cool of the night.

Like plants, animals have adapted to suit the climates of the places where they live. In regions with long, cold winters animals such as musk oxen and polar bears have heavy fur, and their winter coats are generally thicker than those in the summer.

Some animals, such as the arctic fox, grow a white winter coat, which provides camouflage against the snow-covered landscape.

Many animals hibernate in winter – that is, they pass the time in a deep kind of sleep. Before hibernation they eat heartily and store up extra fat to last them through the cold spell, when they cannot find food.

Seasonal Travellers

Many animals solve the problems of harsh winters by migrating. The best-known migrants are birds. Many birds fly north in spring, when there are plenty of insects to provide them with food. They fly south again to tropical lands after they have reared their chicks.

Other birds fly south to Australia and New Zealand in spring, and return to the tropics in the autumn. The arctic tern makes the longest

◄ A camel is adapted to desert life. It has a store of fat in the hump on its back, and can go for days without drinking. Its feet are large and do not sink into the sand. Long, curly eyelashes protect its eyes.

▲ The ermine, also called the stoat, is one of many animals that grows a white coat in winter. In its summer coat it would show against the snow.

▼ The dormouse hibernates in winter when food is scarce.

journeys of all. It spends the northern summer in the Arctic, then when winter comes it flies south to the Antarctic peninsula to enjoy the southern summer.

In desert lands animals have to contend with heat rather than cold. Many animals, such as the jerboas of the Sahara and the kangaroo rats of the North American deserts, burrow into the sand to shield themselves from the heat of the Sun, emerging at night to hunt for seeds.

◄ White storks gather ready to migrate. Many birds spend the winter months in warm lands, then fly to cooler places to nest and have their young.

5: CHANGES IN CLIMATE

Studying Climate Changes

▲ A Nilometer on the River Nile at Aswan.

Old Instruments

Instruments for measuring weather conditions have existed for less than 400 years. The thermometer was invented in 1592, the barometer in 1644, the rain-gauge and wind gauge in the 1600s.

An older and simpler instrument was a Nilometer. These are gauges that were carved in stone at intervals along the banks of the River Nile in ancient Egypt. They measured how high the river rose at the time of the annual floods. Some still survive.

We can see climate changes going on now. An important example of these is the behaviour of the **monsoon** winds, which bring the rain each year on which the countries of southern Asia depend.

If the monsoons fail to bring rain, crops do not grow, and people starve. But world wind patterns are altering. Since the 1960s the seasonal rains have repeatedly failed over large parts of Africa, causing famines.

Changes in the Past

If we understand what has happened in the past, we may be able to learn what is likely to happen in the future. The scientific study of weather and climate began no more than 300 years ago, but fortunately there are plenty of

references to the weather in old books, diaries and other documents.

With their aid climatologists have been able to piece together a jigsaw-like picture of weather in Europe for at least a thousand years, and in China for five thousand years.

Trees are a great help in studying past climates. A tree adds a ring to its trunk for every year it lives, a thin ring in dry years, a thick ring in wet ones. By comparing ring patterns in old recently-felled trees with those in timber from buildings, scientists have built up records for several thousand years.

Buried Clues

Other clues to the past lie buried in the ground, and are found by **archaeologists** and **geologists**.

The mud at the bottom of lakes often preserves plant debris such as **pollen** which shows whether warm-climate or cold-climate plants grew around the lakes in past centuries.

Cores taken from the ocean bed contain the **fossilized** shells of ancient sea-animals. Such remains often show the temperature of the sea-water at the time the animals were alive.

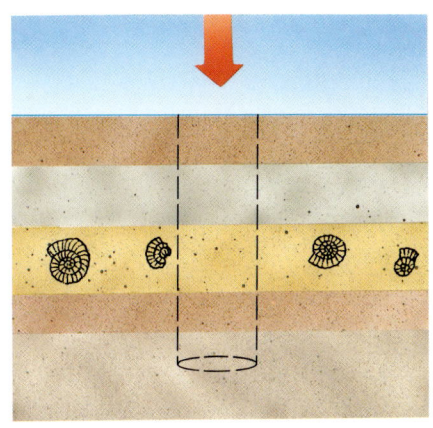

▲ A cylindrical core is drilled down through layers of sedimentary rocks, formed from mud and sand laid down millions of years ago. By studying the fossils and other traces of plant and animal remains found in the rocks, scientists can tell what climate existed when they were deposited.

▼ The rings seen in the stump of this cedar tree vary in width – indicating changes in rainfall from year to year.

◄ This scene near Bermer in western India shows climate changes of today. Because of the failure of the monsoon rains, sand dunes cover land where farmers grew crops only four years before this picture was taken.

Ice Ages

The Evidence

There are several clues to the ice ages of the past. Layers in **sedimentary rocks** – that is, those made up of fragments deposited in water over millions of years – show that at different times in the past there were plants growing, while other layers have no plant remains.

Glaciers have carved out deep valleys (including the fjords of Norway, which are flooded valleys) and left scars on the rocks. They have also carried down silt and rocks, and deposited them.

At several periods during the past 1,000 million years ice has covered large areas of the Earth's land surface. We refer to these periods as **ice ages**. The ice ages we know most about are those of the last 2,000,000 years of Earth history, called the **Quaternary period**.

Even today about ten per cent of the total land is covered by ice. But at various times during the Quaternary period, ice covered roughly 25 per cent of the land.

The Ice Cap

Northern Europe, Siberia and North America had a thick cap of ice, and looked like Antarctica does today. At one stage, in Europe the ice covered Denmark and Germany and reached almost to Moscow, while in North America the ice covered all of Canada, and reached as far south as Kansas and Nebraska.

In the southern hemisphere an ice sheet reached 1,700 km north in Argentina and Chile, and another capped New Zealand.

During this time it is thought that the ice retreated and advanced 17 times, so there were 17 major changes of climate. The periods of maximum ice are known as **glacials**, and the warmer periods in between as **interglacials**. These periods take their name from glaciers.

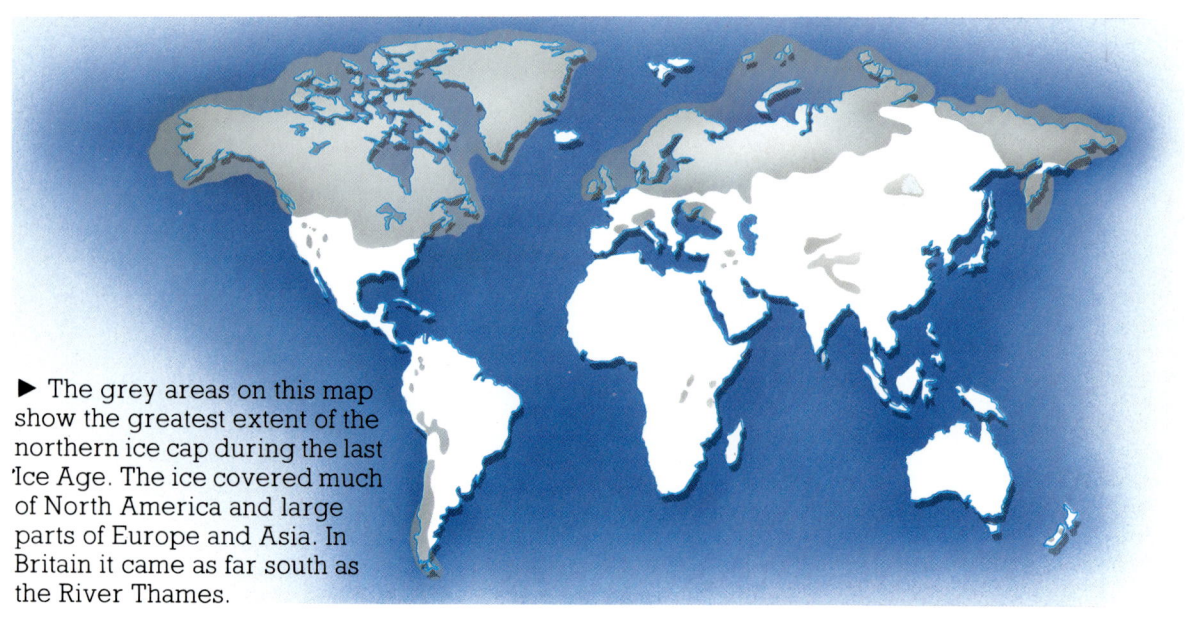

► The grey areas on this map show the greatest extent of the northern ice cap during the last Ice Age. The ice covered much of North America and large parts of Europe and Asia. In Britain it came as far south as the River Thames.

◀ Grisdale, in the Lake District of north-western England, was carved out by a glacier during the last Ice Age. Its U-shape is typical of valleys formed in this way.

Where We Are Now

On average, each glaciation lasted between 40,000 and 60,000 years, while the interglacials lasted between 10,000 and 40,000 years. We are now in an interglacial which began about 10,000 years ago. The climate in Europe is about 5°C warmer than during a glacial period.

During the coldest times so much water was locked up in the ice cap that the level of the oceans dropped by 100 metres. There was dry land between Siberia and Alaska, and the British Isles were joined to continental Europe.

▼ *Glacier d'Arpette* in the Swiss Alps is a glacier of today – a slow moving river of ice. The stones and debris at its side are called moraine. This is also found at the end of the glacier, where melting ice forms a river of water.

Climate in Early Times

▶ This map shows the area of the Fertile Crescent, where farming began about 10,000 years ago. It extended from the Mediterranean Sea through the land between the rivers Euphrates and Tigris to the Persian Gulf. Our modern wheat is descended from the wild wheat which grew in the areas marked.

Radiocarbon Dating

One of the greatest tools of the scientists investigating the climate of the past is the technique known as **radio-carbon dating**. It works like this:

Some of the **atoms** of the element carbon are broken down by **cosmic rays** from the Sun, and become **radioactive**. All living things absorb carbon, including these radioactive atoms. After they die, the radioactive atoms slowly decay at a constant rate.

Scientists can measure the amount of radiocarbon left in, say, a piece of timber, and estimate roughly how old it is. In effect, the radioactive atoms act as a calendar.

The movement and activities of early peoples are a very good indication of the climate in which they lived. The earliest people arrived in Australia and North America during the Ice Age. One of the oldest human records of the climate comes from the cave paintings in France and Spain, made towards the end of the Ice Age. People hunted deer, mammoths and rhinoceroses in Europe.

The development of agriculture in the Middle East happened around 10,000 years ago, about the time the ice was in full retreat. The climate was growing warmer, and it would seem that species of wild wheat had seeded themselves in the Fertile Crescent, the region of western Asia where civilization began. This wheat could be cultivated.

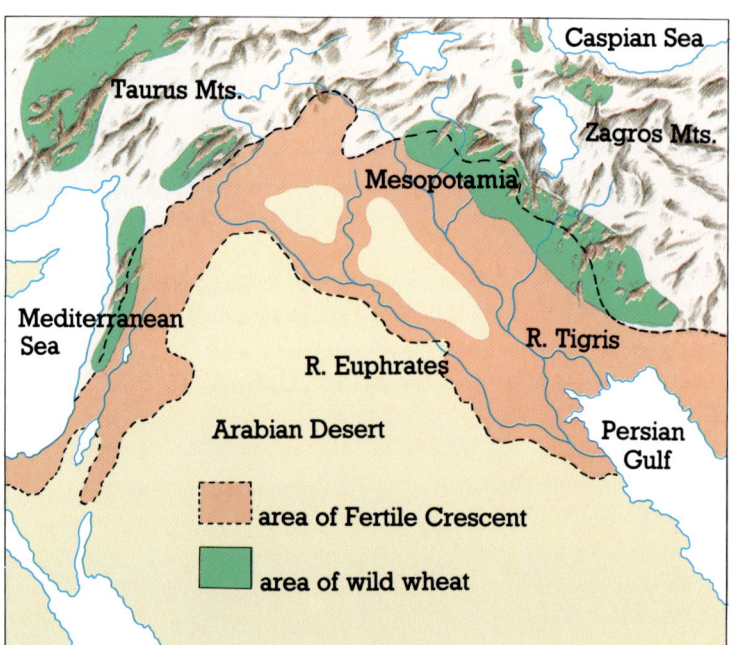

The Warm Centuries

The two or three thousand years before Christ seem to have been the warmest time since the Ice Age ended. Northern China had its warmest time about 5,000 years ago, when subtropical plants and animals flourished there. Bamboo grew much further north than it does today, and there were warm-weather animals such as elephants.

In Northern Europe people enjoyed more clear skies than they do today, to judge by the number of stone circles, such as those on the Outer Hebrides and Orkney Islands, that were probably used, amongst other things, as **astronomical observatories**.

Changes

Warmer weather continued in Europe through Roman times. But climates are never consistent: there were still very cold years and elsewhere some long term changes took place.

The Indus River Valley civilization covered a large area of Pakistan and northwest India. Its two chief cities, Harappa and Mohenjo-Daro, were the centre of a region which had considerable rainfall. The Indus Valley people flourished between 2500 BC and 1700 BC but the rains began to fail. The region today is largely arid, with no more than 250 mm of rain a year.

From about 1700 to 1300 BC a severe climatic change took place in the Americas. There was a rapid cooling in the Rocky Mountains, California, and Central and South America.

▲ The Ring of Brodgar in Orkney was erected about 4,500 years ago. Its stones' position reflect the movement of the moon, suggesting that it was used to watch the night skies.

▲ The remains of the city of Mohenjo-Daro in the Indus River Valley of Pakistan lie amid scrub and semi-desert. When the city flourished more than 4,000 years ago the area had plenty of water and good farm land.

Climate from the Middle Ages

A warm period began in the northern hemisphere in the AD 300s. South of a line running through the northern coast of the Mediterranean Sea in Europe and the Virginia-North Carolina border in the United States, the weather stayed warm, and even grew warmer, for several hundred years.

Climatologists think that this warm weather influenced the growth of the Mayan Empire in North America, and led to the drying up of once good farmland in the Middle East.

Further north the climate grew colder again for some while, but had warmed up once more by AD 1000, when the Viking Leif Eriksson made his historic voyage to 'Vinland' on the coast of North America.

1

2

3

4

Frost Fair Facts

A well documented guide to European climate in the past is the River Thames in England.

Old London Bridge across the Thames had 19 arches on heavy pillars, and acted rather like a dam. So when ice did form it piled up rapidly, and the river was more likely to freeze.

The greatest freeze-up came in the winter of 1683-4, at the height of the Little Ice Age, when the ice was 28 cm thick. A huge Frost Fair was held on the ice, with hundreds of stalls. The Thames has not frozen since Old London Bridge was demolished in 1831, having frozen 30 times during the bridge's 600-year life.

The Little Ice Age

Then the cold returned. Accounts show that the period from about 1400 to 1800 was colder than before or since, and climatologists call it the Little Ice Age.

The onset of the Little Ice Age saw the end of the **Norse** settlement in Greenland, established in the late 900s by Leif's father, Erik the Red. Erik gave that chilly island its unlikely name to encourage settlers, but it is probable that Greenland was much warmer and greener when he first went there.

Records of wine harvests in France and Germany date from around 1300. These give a good indication of the extremes of weather (both hot and cold) that the Little Ice Age brought. Other clues are the abandoning of farmland in Scandinavia in the late 17th century as the weather became more severe.

There was a warm period about the middle of the 1800s, but cold weather set in again in 1879, bringing famine to China and India.

The climate began warming again in the 1920s, although the Baltic Sea froze between Sweden and the Danish Island of Sjaelland in 1924. But in the past hundred years the climate has been less variable. Most of the changes have been slight or just temporary.

5

6

◀ Some incidents from the past 2,000 years showing changes in the climate in the northern hemisphere.

1   The Mayan civilization of North and Central America reached its height between AD 250 and AD 900, at a time when the climate was warm.

2   When Erik the Red settled in Greenland about 982 the climate was reasonably warm – enough for Erik to call the island green. But the settlement died out in the 1400s when the climate turned colder.

3   There was increasingly unsettled weather in the build up to the Little Ice Age. In the fourteenth century, huge storms led to the flooding of large areas of low-lying land in northern Europe.

4   The largest of the many Frost Fairs held in London on the River Thames, particularly during the Little Ice Age. This picture is based on a painting made in 1684.

5   The blight which attacked the potato crop in Ireland in 1846 spread rapidly because the weather had turned very warm and humid.

6   The Baltic Sea froze over during a cold climate spell in the late 1800s and again in 1924. People could walk across the ice from Sweden to Denmark.

49

The Moving Deserts

▼ The areas coloured yellow on this map show the world's deserts as they are today. The darker areas are the regions showing signs of becoming deserts. Some of this desertification is the result of natural causes, but human activity is also responsible.

Just as the cave paintings of Europe tell us something of the climate of the continent in the ice age, so rock paintings in the Sahara show how the ending of the ice age led to the growth of the desert.

The paintings were made about 5,500 years ago in the Tassili Mountains of southern Algeria. They show many animals no longer found in the Sahara, including antelopes, crocodiles, deer, elephants and giraffes.

One of the most remarkable drawings shows men hunting hippotamuses from canoes. So the now-dry Sahara was wet then.

Grasslands covered much of the Sahara, and there were many rivers. Lake Chad was many times its present size and its water level was as much as 40 metres higher than today.

The Sahara's change from a green and pleasant land to the world's largest desert coincided with the thawing of northern Europe. Rainfall moved further south, leaving the region mainly dry.

The Sahara is still moving south. The Sahel, at the southern edge of the Sahara, is a region in which the desert gives way to savanna, grassland with trees. The annual rainfall in the region is very unpredictable, ranging from 40 mm to nearly 170 mm in the northern Sahel,

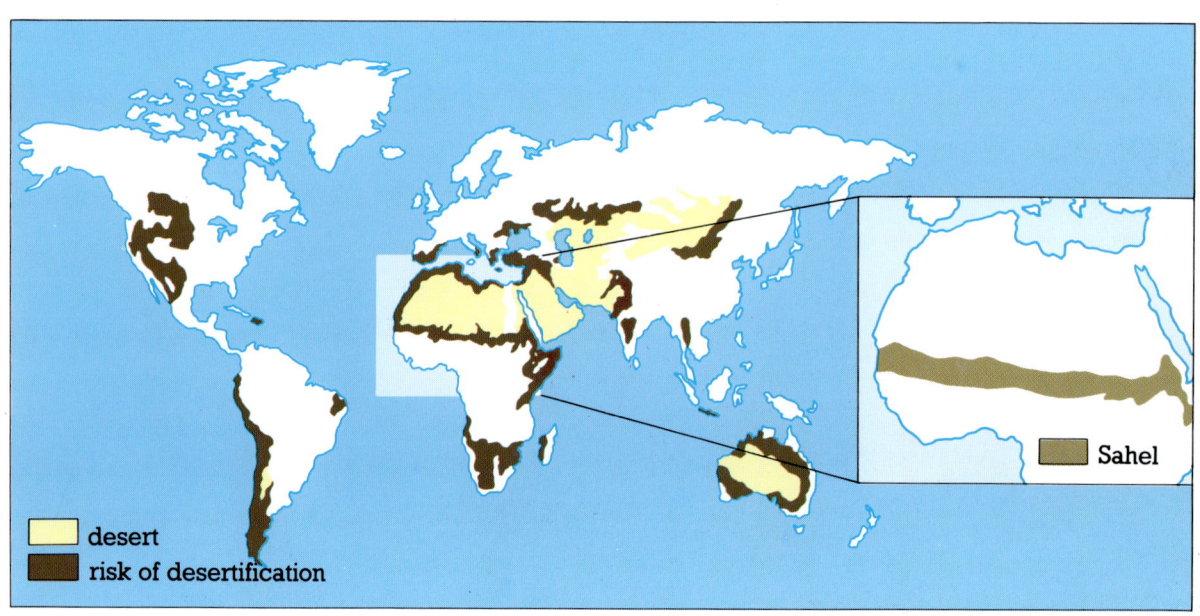

desert

risk of desertification

Sahel

and becoming much wetter in the southern Sahel. The desert is moving slowly into the northern Sahel. This is one of the reasons for the disastrous famines in Ethiopia and Sudan in recent years.

As the map shows, there are other areas in the world in danger of **desertification**. This is partly through natural causes, such as prolonged drought, but people have over-used already poor farmland and cleared vegetation which has made the problem far worse.

▲ One of the rock paintings in the Tassili Mountains in Algeria, showing men tending cattle in an area that is now part of the Sahara. It suggests that, in the past, the area must have been greener to support cattle grazing.

Did You Know?

The desert sand of the Sahara in Africa sometimes blows over Europe, including the British Isles. It leaves a fine red dust on cars and other surfaces, and in wet weather produces what is called red rain.

◀ Herding cattle towards green pastures in Niger, in the Sahel. This is one of the areas where unpredictable rainfall is causing the Sahara to spread.

6: PEOPLE AND CLIMATE

People's Influence on Climate

Modern people, *Homo sapiens sapiens* to give them their scientific name, have been around for at least 35,000 years.

As we have seen, climate, and changes in climate, have affected how and where they live. For most of that time it has not worked the other way: people have had no effect on climate.

In the past 200 years things have changed dramatically. In 1800 the world had fewer than 1,000 million people. By the year 2000 the population is expected to top 6,500 million.

Polluting the Air

In that time the world has become industrialized. Vast quantities of chemicals and other pollutants are now pumped into the air. People are changing the Earth's atmosphere, and in doing so they are changing its climate.

One of the earliest changes was in the climate of large towns. The heat from houses heated by fires made the air around towns warmer, and smoke from those fires hung like a shroud over them.

◄ The Dust Bowl in the Great Plains of America in the 1930s.

The Dust Bowl

Even changing the type of plants that grow in an area can alter the climate. In the 1930s farmers in the Great Plains of America ploughed up the natural grasses which bound the soil together to plant crops such as wheat.

This was all right in wet weather, but in long dry spells the surface soil of the exposed land was blown away by the wind, creating what was known as the Dust Bowl. In time this could produce a desert landscape.

◄ ◄ Far left, dead trees in the Black Forest of Germany, swathed in the acid fog that has helped to kill them.

▼ Smog blankets Mexico City, the world's largest city. It lies high above sea-level in a valley, which traps pollution from industry and cars.

Smog

Smoke combined with fog led to heavy outbreaks of smog. Some of the densest smogs occurred in London, where they became known as 'London Particulars'. Similar smogs occurred in Düsseldorf and Berlin. The problem in these three places was recognized and dealt with. However, more recently many cities have become affected, including Mexico City, Los Angeles, Bangkok and Cairo.

A different kind of climate change results from cutting down trees, either for timber or to clear land for growing crops and building. Trees absorb the gas carbon dioxide, which people and animals breathe out, and give out oxygen, which people and animals breathe in. By destroying the forests, the balance of oxygen and carbon dioxide in the atmosphere is changing. Clearing trees also changes the albedo of an area.

Forests used to cover about 60 per cent of the land. Now they cover less than half that amount. The **tropical rain forests** are being cleared at the rate of 41 hectares a minute.

The Green-house Effect

Smoke billows out of chimneys ▲ at the Anshan Steel and Iron Factory in China. The carbon dioxide produced by this kind of heavy industry is among the main causes of the greenhouse effect which is believed to be making the Earth grow warmer.

What Are CFCs?

CFCs are compounds of three chemical elements, carbon, chlorine and fluorine. They are inert substances, colourless with hardly any smell. They are nonflammable. They are manufactured under a number of trade names such as Arctons, Freons, Geons and Genetrons.

Besides their use in aerosols, they are used as cooling fluids in air conditioners and refrigerators and escape into the atmosphere when such apparatus is broken up. CFCs are also used in insulating and packaging foams.

Coal, oil and natural gas are all fuels which we extract from the ground. Millions of years ago, plants of prehistoric forests decayed and formed coal. Tiny plants and animals that once floated in the seas decayed to form oil and natural gas. For this reason, coal, oil and natural gas are called fossil fuels.

When we burn fossil fuels they give off quantities of the gas carbon dioxide. There has always been a small amount of carbon dioxide in the Earth's atmosphere, but since the start of the **Industrial Revolution** in the 1700s the amount has increased. We do not know exactly by how much.

Trapping Radiation

Carbon dioxide allows the Sun's rays and warmth to reach the surface of the Earth, but hinders the escape of heat from the Earth.

Other gases that act in the same way are **nitrous oxide**, small quantities of which are produced by burning fossil fuels, and **chlorofluorocarbons (CFCs)**, which are used in aerosols and refrigerators.

Those gases are all called 'greenhouse gases', because they act like the glass of a greenhouse. Just as the atmosphere in a greenhouse is warmer than the air outside, so the surface of the Earth and the lower layers of its atmosphere gradually become warmer. This is called the greenhouse effect.

Warming Up

Scientists have detected signs that the Earth is warming up. In Europe glaciers flowing down mountainsides are growing shorter, and there are signs that the southern hemisphere is also growing warmer.

The Earth may be having one of its warmer periods anyway, but most scientists believe that human activity is increasing the greenhouse effect. In view of the evidence, we cannot take the chance that we are not responsible for this change.

The Likely Results

If the greenhouse effect goes on, the results for the world's climates are likely to be dramatic. The ice caps will melt, and the sea level will rise. Low-lying coastal areas will be flooded.

Regions with permanently frozen soil, such as Siberia and northern Canada, may become warm and pleasant places to live.

We can also expect changes in the pattern of rainfall. Some regions will get less than they do now, others more. The Sahara might become green again, while other parts become deserts.

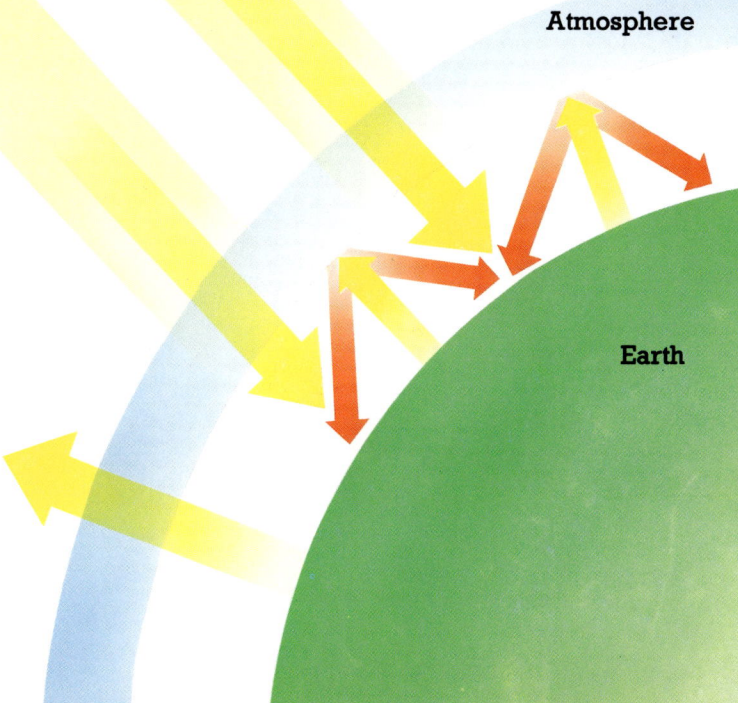

Sun's rays

Atmosphere

Earth

▶ This diagram shows how rays from the Sun penetrate the Earth's atmosphere. But too much carbon dioxide in the air can hinder heat from the surface of the Earth radiating back into space, trapping it inside the Earth's atmosphere – the greenhouse effect. Some scientists fear that over the next hundred years the temperature of the Earth could rise by as much as 5°C.

The Ozone Layer

The atmosphere forms a shield to protect the Earth from the most harmful rays of the Sun. One of the most important parts of that shield is the **ozone** layer, which is between 10 km and 60 km above the ground. This layer absorbs ultraviolet rays.

Ozone, a bluish gas, is a form of oxygen. Most oxygen exists as a **molecule** in which two oxygen atoms are firmly bonded together. Ozone has a third atom, loosely bonded.

It has a sharp smell, which you can sometimes detect near electrical machines and in thunderstorms. Ozone also exists nearer the ground, as a component of smog.

▶ These diagrams show how the ozone hole – the area of ozone depletion – over Antarctica has increased since it was first discovered. The upper diagram shows the approximate area in the early 1980s, and the lower picture the situation in 1989.

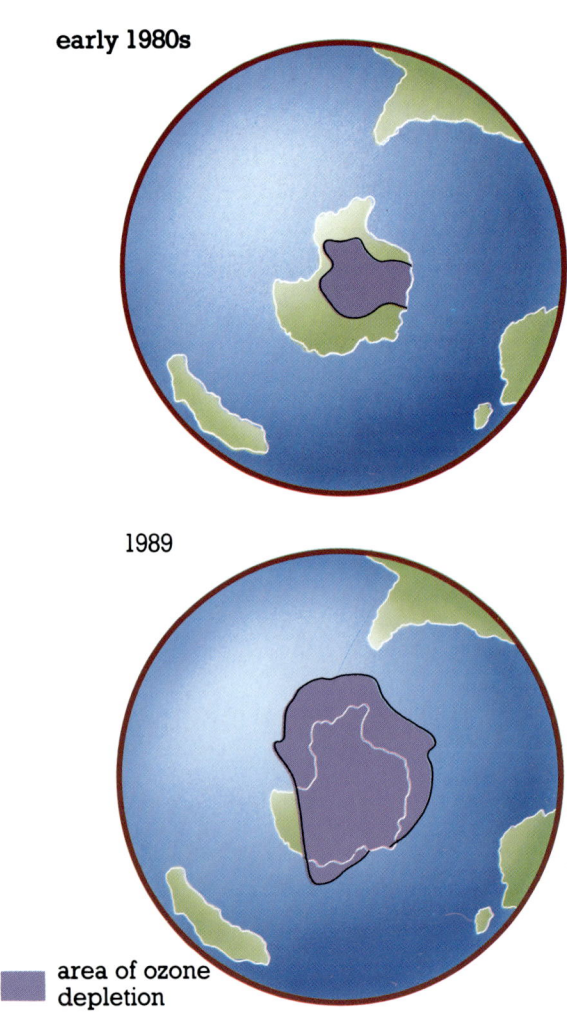

early 1980s

1989

area of ozone depletion

The Dangers

Fortunately the Antarctic ozone hole is over an area where there are very few people. If the ozone layer is seriously thinned over other places these could be the results:

More people could develop skin cancers, cataracts and blindness;

Some infectious diseases could spread more easily;

Plants of the **plankton** could be affected, which could upset the **food chain** in the oceans;

Acid smog might form;

Food plants such as rice might well yield smaller crops.

Years of Tests

British scientists based in Antarctica began measuring the amount of ozone in the ozone layer about 1960. During the early 1980s, they made an unpleasant discovery: there was a hole in the layer, right over Antarctica each spring (September to October).

Since then the hole has appeared every spring, and it tends to grow bigger each year. By 1988 it covered the whole of Antarctica, and affected parts of Australia and New Zealand.

Something was attacking the ozone and destroying it. Among the culprits appear to be the chlorofluorocarbon gases. The ozone hole has appeared since CFCs became widely used.

A treaty signed by 14 leading countries in 1987 agreed to cut the production and use of CFCs. But by the time it came into effect in January 1989 the CFCs were attacking the ozone layer over the Arctic, too, and causing a thinning of the layer in other places.

If the ozone layer is seriously reduced the Earth's climate may warm up, adding to the greenhouse effect. Unfortunately CFCs last a long time – up to 140 years – so the problem of the ozone layer is likely to be with us for many years.

Friendly Cans?

An aerosol is a mixture of very fine liquid or solid particles with a gas. Clouds and smoke are natural aerosols. The ones you use in cans for spraying such things as oven cleaners, paint and perfume are manufactured.

Not all aerosols are powered by CFC gases. More and more makers are producing spray cans that use other, safer gases. Look out for the label 'Ozone Friendly' on an aerosol before you buy one.

▲ The British Antarctic Survey Station in Western Antarctica, where scientists first detected the ozone hole.

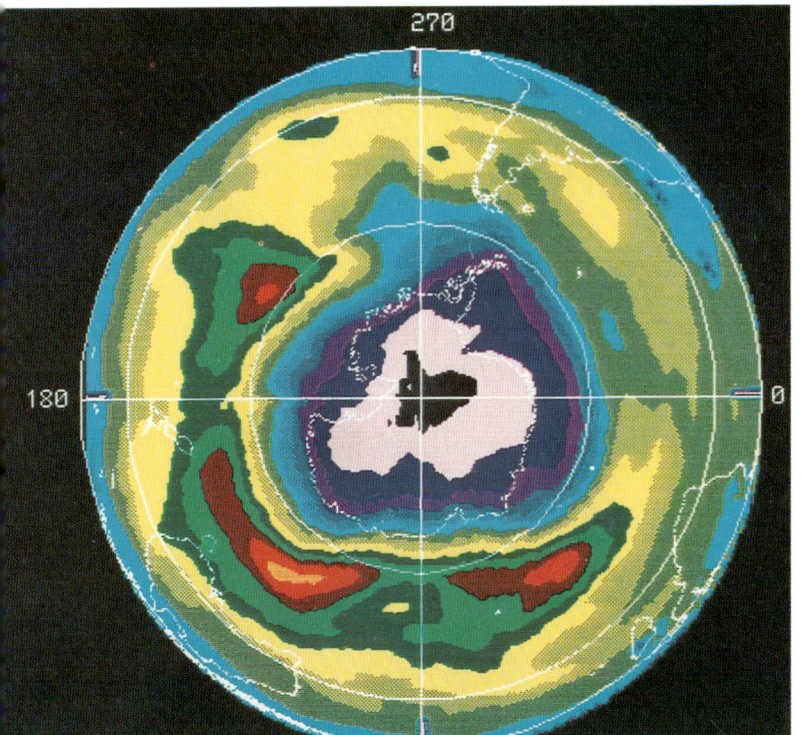

◄ This picture, taken by the US Nimbus-7 satellite, shows how scientists observe the ozone layer. It was taken in October 1987, the Antarctic spring, the time of year when the hole is largest. Black is maximum depletion of ozone, and the pink and purple areas show slightly less depleted areas.

Climate in the Future

▶ A rusting, rotting fishing fleet lies on dry land. A few years ago this was the shore of the Aral Sea, but the water is now several kilometres away. Between 1961 and 1989 the Aral Sea has shrunk by more than a third, from 66,000 square kilometres to 36,500 square kilometres. The water has become more salty, and most of the sea's fish have died.

Sunny England?

If the climate of Europe does turn warmer, we may expect that the beaches of England will become as sunny and popular as those of the Mediterranean countries are now.

However, if the ice caps start to melt and the sea level rises, southern England may be flooded for some kilometres inland. It is already sinking slowly: the whole island of Great Britain is tilting up towards the north as the land adjusts itself after the melting of the ice that once covered so much of it. So there might be some very different seaside resorts in future centuries.

Whatever the effects of human activity, it seems certain that the world's climate is changing. But it is hard to see if it is warming or cooling down. We may still be in the middle of the interglacial that began 10,000 years ago, or it may be coming to an end.

The disastrous droughts and famines that have beset Africa have persisted long enough to suggest that they are part of a permanent change. At the moment we cannot tell how much people have contributed to this change.

The Action Needed

The most important thing about climate changes is to see how they are affecting the world's food supplies. We have become accustomed to being able to grow ample food in places like the plains of Europe and America.

Now we need to watch the climate to see whether the traditional 'granaries of the world' will remain able to supply enough food for the hungry billions of the coming years. In all this the study of past climates can help us to see what future climates may be like.

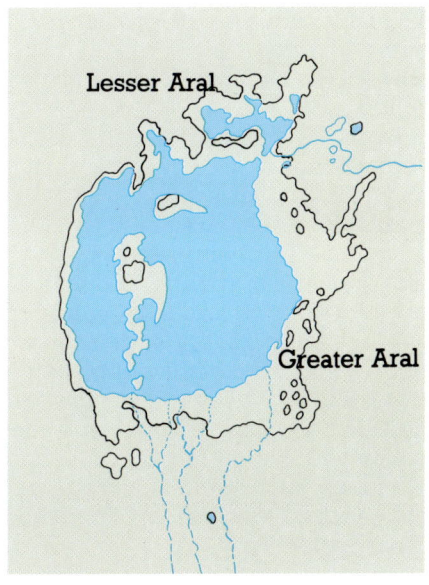

▲ This diagram shows the boundaries of the Aral Sea in 1961 and 1989. By 1989 it had split into two – the Greater and Lesser Aral Seas.

However, in taking steps to safeguard food crops in one area we must be careful not to do anything to upset the climate or the environment in another. The Russians have already run into trouble by drawing water from the rivers that feed the Aral and Caspian Seas in order to supply industry and farmland.

As a result, the Aral Sea is drying up fast, creating vast areas of poisoned wasteland. The level of the Caspian Sea has also dropped alarmingly. Because less fresh water is flowing into the Caspian, it is becoming too salty, with harmful effects on fish and other life in it.

To counter this, the Russians are planning to divert water from the major rivers, such as the Ob and the Yenisey, that flow into the Arctic Ocean. But without their fresh water ice might not form on the Arctic Ocean.

If that happened the whole climate of the area might grow as much as 10°C warmer. This in turn would be liable to divert northward the winds which bring rain to Europe and central Asia. It is necessary to think several moves ahead when meddling with the climate.

▲ Famines, caused by lack of rainfall, are affecting large areas of Africa. Here relief workers are providing a porridge of sorghum milk, oil and soya for starving women and children in Mali.

Glossary

air masses: bodies of air that move constantly over the globe.

albedo: the amount of light that a surface reflects.

altitude: the height of a place above sea level.

anticyclone: an area of high pressure where winds spiral outward.

archaeologist: a person who studies the past by examining ruins and remains.

asteroid: one of about 30,000 minor planets that orbit the Sun between Mars and Jupiter.

astronomical observatory: place where people study the stars and planets.

atmosphere: the layer of various gases (mostly nitrogen and oxygen) that surrounds the Earth.

atoms: the 'building blocks' of chemical elements; each element is made up of identical atoms which are different from those of any other element.

axis: a line about which something rotates; the Earth appears to rotate around an axis that cuts through it at the **poles**.

carbon dioxide: a colourless, odourless gas given out by animals and absorbed by plants.

chlorofluorocarbons (CFCs): gases made up from chlorine, fluorine and carbon, which damage the **ozone** layer.

communications satellite: satellite that sends radio and television signals around the world.

computer network: two or more computers linked by cable or radio.

condense: to change from a gas or vapour to a liquid or solid.

contour lines: lines on a map that join together points of equal height.

cores: cylinder-shaped samples of rock or soil taken with a hollow drill.

cosmic rays: rays from the Sun and other sources in space.

craters: hollows left by the impact of **meteorites** or the eruption of volcanoes.

crystals: solids with regular shapes, for example sugar or snowflakes.

cyclone: an area of low pressure where winds spiral inward.

data: facts, measurements or observations (singular *datum*).

dense: describes how heavy something is in relation to its size.

depression: another name for a **cyclone**.

desertification: changing to a barren desert of land that in the past could support more varied vegetation.

ellipse: a shape like a flattened circle; sometimes called an oval.

evaporation: changing from a liquid or a solid to a **vapour**.

food chain: a series of plants and animals, each of which feeds on another in the chain.

fossilized: what happens when the remains of a plant or animal is preserved in rock.

fossil fuels: coal, oil and natural gas; formed from long-dead plants and animals.

front: point where a **frontal zone** reaches the ground.

frontal zone: boundary between two **air masses**, one being warmer than the other.

genetically: relating to genes, the tiny units that determine what animals (and people) inherit from their parents.

geologist: a person who studies the Earth's beginning, structure and what it is made from.

glacial: a period when large areas of land were covered by ice; often called an **ice age**.

ground hog: a North American animal of the squirrel family; also called a woodchuck.

helium: a very light, colourless, non-flammable gas; used to float balloons.

hemisphere: half a globe. The Earth is divided into the northern and southern hemispheres by the Equator.

high: a short term for an area of high pressure or **anticyclone**.

Himalayas: huge mountain chain north of India; has the world's highest peaks.

hurricane: a tropical **cyclone** producing a violent storm.

humidity: the amount of water **vapour** in the air.

hydrogen: a gas, the lightest chemical element.

ice age: a period when large areas of land were covered by ice.

ice caps: sheets of ice covering large areas of land, especially in Antarctica and Greenland.

Industrial Revolution: the development of large-scale industry, which began in Britain around 1750.

interglacial: a warm period between **glacials**.

isobars: lines linking points of equal pressure.

land mass: area of land, usually large; often used to describe the Eurasian and American continents.

latitudes: regions lying north or south of the Equator, marked by imaginary lines. The higher the latitude, the further away it is from the Equator.

lichen: a plant consisting of a fungus and an alga living together. It can live in extreme temperatures.

lows: a short term for an area of low pressure or **cyclone**.

magnetic field: the area of force surrounding a magnet.

mercury: a silver-coloured metal, which is a liquid at normal temperatures.

meteorite: lump of metallic or rocky material that lands on the Earth from outer space.

Middle Ages: period of history between ancient and modern, about AD 400-1500.

molecule: unit of matter containing two or more **atoms**.

monsoon: a wind that changes direction according to the season; it also describes the rains it brings to certain parts of the world in summer.

nitrous oxide: a colourless, odourless gas, used in aerosols.

Norse: relating to ancient Scandinavia and the Viking culture.

occluded: a term describing a front which lies between two cold **air masses**.

orbit: the path of one planet or other heavenly body round another.

ozone: a colourless gas whose molecules contain three oxygen **atoms**.

Pennines: sometimes known as the backbone of England, a range of high hills that stretches from the north southwards to the middle of the country.

pigment: substance which gives an animal or vegetable its colour.

plankton: minute plants and animals which drift in the sea's upper waters.

poles: the two points (north and south) marking the ends of the Earth's **axis**.

pollen: a fine powdery substance produced by flowering or cone-bearing plants.

precipitation: a general name for the various forms of rain, hail and snow.

prevailing wind: the most common wind (and its direction) to blow in a particular area.

Quaternary period: the most recent period of Earth history, beginning about 2 million years ago.

radar: a device that measures the distance to an object and its movement by bouncing radio waves off it.

radiation: the flow of particles and rays, such as light and radio waves.

radiation balance: the overall heating effect of the Sun on the Earth, taking into account the heat lost from the Earth at the same time.

radioactive: giving out atomic energy.

radiocarbon dating: dating an object by the amount of **radioactive** material it contains.

sedimentary rock: rock, such as sandstone, that was formed by deposits of tiny particles from other rock.

solar flare: a powerful eruption from the Sun's surface.

solar wind: the flow of electrically charged particles from the Sun.

static electricity: electricity that does not flow, unlike an electric current.

statistics: a collection of **data** which can be classified and analysed.

sulphur dioxide: a colourless, poisonous gas, produced from rotting plant or animal matter, or by volcanoes.

sunspots: periodic spots that appear on the surface of the Sun, showing extra activity within.

temperate: having a climate between polar and tropical.

tides: the regular movements of the sea.

tornado: a sudden, violent storm with a funnel-shaped cloud; also called a twister.

tree line: a line beyond which the climate is too cold for trees to grow.

tropical rain forest: forest in the **tropics** where there is heavy rainfall.

tropics: band around the Earth either side of the Equator where the climate is warm or hot all the year round.

vacuum: a space entirely empty of anything, including air. Other matter will always try to fill a vacuum.

vapour: particles of moisture or solids forming clouds or smoke.

visibility: the clearness and range of sight in the **atmosphere**; the distance it is possible to see.

weather buoys: floating objects anchored at sea, carrying weather instruments.

weather system: a connected pattern of highs and lows and the weather conditions relating to it.

Index

A **Bold** number shows the entry is illustrated on that page. The same page often has writing about the entry too.

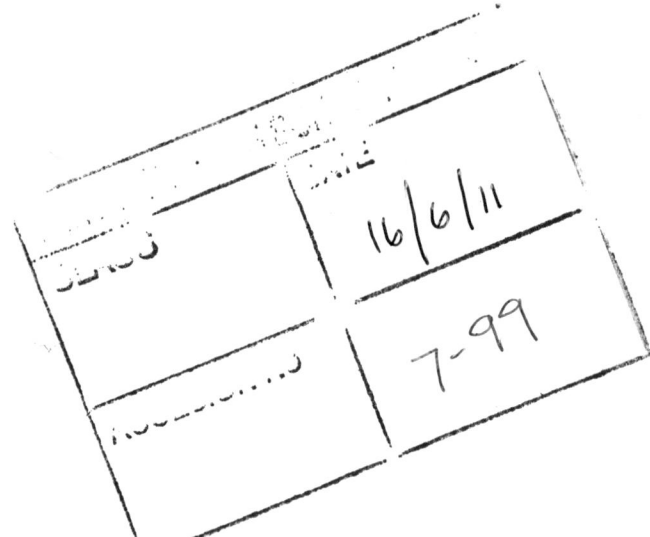